W9-BYL-474

MARK TWAIN

Legendary Writer and Humorist

Lynda Pflueger

Enslow Publishers, Inc.

40 Industrial Road	PO Box 38
Box 398	Aldershot
Berkeley Heights, NJ 07922	Hants GU12 6BP
USA	UK

http://www.enslow.com

To my father

Library of Congress Cataloging-in-Publication Data

Pflueger, Lynda.
    Mark Twain : legendary writer and humorist / Lynda Pflueger.
       p. cm. — (Historical American biographies)
    Includes bibliographical references (p.) and index.
    Summary: A biography of the American humorist and writer whose
writing greatly reflected the events of his life particularly his boyhood in
Hannibal, Missouri.
    ISBN 0-7660-1093-7
    1. Twain, Mark, 1835–1910—Juvenile literature. 2. Humorists,
American—19th century—Biography—Juvenile literature. 3. Authors,
American—19th century—Biography—Juvenile literature. [1. Twain,
Mark, 1835–1910. 2. Authors, American.] I. Title. II. Series.
PS1331.P52   1999
818'.409—dc21
[B]   98-31293
                               CIP
                               AC

Printed in the United States of America

10 9 8 7 6 5 4 3 2 1

To Our Readers:
All Internet addresses in this book were active and appropriate when we
went to press. Any comments or suggestions can be sent by e-mail to
Comments@enslow.com or to the address on the back cover.

Illustration Credits: Enslow Publishers, Inc., pp. 38, 60; Library of
Congress, pp. 4, 9, 31, 66, 75, 82, 84, 102, 105, 110, 112; Mark Twain
Project—Bancroft Library, pp. 21, 24, 47, 61, 78, 109; The Mark Twain
House, Hartford, CT, pp. 89, 94.

Cover Illustration: Library of Congress (Inset);
Museum of Fine Arts, Boston/The Hayden Collection (Background).

Boys in a Pasture
1874
Homer, Winslow
U.S., 1836–1910
Oil on Canvas
15 7/8 x 22 7/8 in.
(40.3 cm x 58.1 cm)

CONTENTS

Mark Twain

1

LIFE ON THE MISSISSIPPI

All year long, the sleepy little town of Hannibal, Missouri, on the banks of the Mississippi River, came to life twice a day when the riverboat came to town. As soon as the loud cry of "S-t-e-a-m-boat a-comin'!" was heard, everyone stopped what they were doing and headed for the wharf.[1] As it approached, the riverboat was "a handsome sight" to behold.[2] It was "long and sharp and trim and pretty" and black smoke was "rolling and tumbling" out of its "two tall chimneys."[3] When it docked, a great commotion began on the wharf. People rushed to get aboard, passing people rushing to go ashore. Freight was loaded and unloaded at the same time.

There was a lot of yelling and cursing, and ten minutes later the boat was under way again.

Mark Twain grew up in Hannibal and often witnessed this scene. Using memories of his boyhood experiences, Twain wrote two of his most famous books: *The Adventures of Tom Sawyer*, published in 1876, and *Adventures of Huckleberry Finn*, published in 1885. He used his hometown as the setting for the books, and his boyhood friends and family as models for the characters.

The character of Tom Sawyer was a composite of Mark Twain and a few of his boyhood friends. In the book, Tom is a mischievous boy who plays hooky, tries to get out of doing chores, witnesses a murder, taunts the family cat, falls in love, stages pranks, and takes advantage of his friends. Twain once said that Tom was "all the boy" that he ever knew.[4]

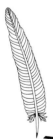

The Mississippi River
The Mississippi River is the second longest river in the United States, flowing 2,348 miles from northern Minnesota to the Gulf of Mexico. The depth of the river ranges from nine feet to one hundred feet. The widest point of the river is near Clinton, Iowa, where, from shore to shore, the river is three and a half miles wide. With the development of steamboats in the early 1800s, the Mississippi became a major transportation route for both passengers and freight.

Tom, with his half brother Sid, was being raised by their aunt Polly. Twain used his mother as a basis for the character of Aunt Polly, but made her more sentimental and less humorous than his mother had been. His younger brother, Henry, was, in part, the model for Sid. Twain also used his rowdy neighbor, Tom Blankenship, as the model for Tom's friend Huckleberry Finn, and Twain's childhood sweetheart, Laura Hawkins, was the basis for the character Becky Thatcher, Tom Sawyer's sweetheart.

In one of the best scenes in the book, Tom has been burdened with the task of whitewashing his aunt's fence as a punishment for coming home late. He tries to talk a young slave boy into doing the job for him, but his aunt catches them and puts an end to their negotiations. Then, one of Tom's friends stops to talk, and Tom comes up with a way to trick him into helping. He pretends he likes what he is doing and does not consider it work. When his friend wants to try his hand at the job, Tom tells him no, saying Aunt Polly is "awful particular about this fence; it's got to be done very careful; I reckon there ain't one boy in a thousand, maybe two thousand, that can do it the way it's got to be done."[5]

Tom's friend pleads to be allowed to paint the fence, but Tom continues to play hard to get. Finally, when his friend offers to trade his half-eaten apple for a chance at the job, Tom gives in. Every

once in a while another of Tom's friends comes along
and wants a chance to paint the fence. Before the
afternoon is over, Tom has traded his fence-painting
job for quite a collection—a kite, a dead rat, twelve
marbles, a piece of blue bottle-glass, a key, fire-
crackers, tadpoles, and a kitten with one eye.[6]

After the success of *The Adventures of Tom
Sawyer*, Twain wrote a sequel. This time he chose
Huckleberry Finn, whom he nicknamed Huck, to be
the main character and narrator of his story. Twain
begins *Adventures of Huckleberry Finn* with Huck
saying, "You don't know about me" unless you have
read *The Adventures of Tom Sawyer*. "That book was
made by Mr. Mark Twain, and he told the truth,
mainly."[7]

Huck is a rambunctious youth who rebels against
authority and sets out on a high-spirited adventure
down the Mississippi River with a runaway slave
named Jim. In one of the most memorable scenes in
the book, Huck struggles with the moral dilemma of
whether he should turn Jim in to the authorities.
Everything he has learned, so far, tells him he should
turn a runaway slave in, or he will go to hell when
he dies. Huck writes a note telling Jim's owner, Miss
Watson, of Jim's whereabouts, but then hesitates
before he mails it. Huck thinks about all the things
Jim has done for him, and how Jim has said Huck is
his best friend and "the *only* one he's got now."[8]
Then Huck starts trembling because he is caught

E·W·Kemble
·1884·

This drawing of Huckleberry Finn by E. W. Kemble appeared in Mark Twain's book Adventures of Huckleberry Finn.

between two things—doing what he has been told is right and betraying a friend. Finally he says, "All right, then, I'll *go* to hell," and tears up the note.[9]

Several million copies of *The Adventures of Tom Sawyer* have been sold. The book has been translated into dozens of languages, and it has never been out of print. In the opinion of many literary critics, *Adventures of Huckleberry Finn* was Mark Twain's masterpiece. The book helped establish Twain as one of the great figures in American literature.

2

EARLY YEARS

M ark Twain" was his pen name, not his real name. His real name was Samuel Langhorne Clemens, and he was the sixth child of Jane Lampton and John Marshall Clemens. His mother was born on June 18, 1803, in Adair County, Kentucky. She was lively and charming, a red-haired beauty who loved to dance and ride horses. Sam's father, the eldest of five children, was born in Campbell County, Virginia, on August 11, 1798. His family moved to Kentucky in 1805.

When John Clemens met Jane Lampton, he was a stern, humorless young attorney who was "always a gentleman" and appeared to have a promising future.[1] After a misunderstanding with her childhood sweetheart, Jane accepted John Clemens's proposal of marriage. They were married on May 6, 1823. For a few years, they lived in Jane's hometown of Columbia, Kentucky. Then they moved to Gainesboro, Tennessee, where their first child, Orion, was born on July 17, 1825. From there, the family drifted across the Cumberland Mountains to Jamestown, Tennessee.

On September 13, 1827, the Clemenses' second child, Pamela, was born. The following year, a boy named Pleasant arrived. He lived only a few months. On May 31, 1830, another daughter, named Margaret, was born. A year later, the family moved to the village of Pall Mall, Tennessee, in search of better farmland. There, their fifth child, Benjamin, was born on June 8, 1832.

Florida, Missouri

Unable to establish a profitable legal practice, John Clemens supported his family on the small income he earned as postmaster of Pall Mall. In 1835, looking westward with dreams of a better life, he moved his family to Florida, Missouri. Several members of Jane's family had settled there, including her father and sister, Patsy Quarles.

Jane Clemens was pregnant when they arrived in Florida. On November 30, 1835, she unexpectedly went into labor two months early. Dr. Thomas Jefferson Chowning was summoned to help with the delivery. The baby boy was small and feeble and his parents doubted he would live. "I could see no promise in him. But I felt it my duty to do the best I could. To raise him if I could," Jane Clemens later wrote.[2] John Clemens named his son Samuel, after his father, and Langhorne, after a close "Virginia friend."[3]

Little Sam or Sammy, as his family called him, clung to life. He grew to be a delicate, somewhat odd, and silent child. He walked in his sleep and was often found in the middle of the night, crying and cold in some dark corner of the house. At other times he was hyperactive and noisy and would begin "swinging his arms into the wind" and then fall down "with shrieks and spasms of laughter and madly roll over and over in the grass."[4]

Hannibal, Missouri

On July 13, 1838, Sam's little brother, Henry, was born. Shortly afterward, his father became dissatisfied with the town of Florida, which had failed to grow as he had expected. In August 1839, when Sam was nearly four years old, his older sister

Halley's Comet
Halley's Comet was visible in the sky when Samuel Langhorne Clemens was born. A comet is a bright object in space that looks like a star with a long tail of light. It travels along an oval path around the sun. Discovered by English astronomer Edmond Halley, Halley's Comet appears in the sky above Earth about every seventy-seven years.

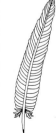

Margaret became ill and suddenly died. A month later, the grieving family moved thirty miles away, to Hannibal, Missouri, on the Mississippi River.

John Clemens sold his property in Florida and with the proceeds bought one fourth of a city block, including a row of shops and a small hotel, in downtown Hannibal. He set up a general store in one of the shops and hired his eldest son, Orion, to work as a clerk.

Shortly after the family arrived in Hannibal, Jane Clemens decided to send Sam to school. Henry was now a toddler, and four-year-old Sam had to be watched every minute because he would often run away, usually toward the river. She hoped the discipline he would learn in school would help settle him down.

There were no public schools in Missouri at the time, so she enrolled Sam in Elizabeth Horr's private school, located in a small log house at the south end of Main Street. Horr charged twenty-five cents per student per week and taught manners, reading, recitation, long division, and spelling up to the third-grade level. Each school day began with a prayer and a reading from a chapter in the New Testament of the Bible.

Sam was not in the classroom very long before he broke one of the school rules. Horr warned him not to do it again. A short time later, he broke the rule again, and she sent him outside to find a switch for her to use to punish him. Sam came back with a small wood shaving that was totally inadequate for the job. "Samuel Langhorne Clemens," Horr said, "I am ashamed of you!"[5] Then she sent another student out to bring back a switch and gave Sam a whipping with it.

Later, Sam went home and told his mother that "he did not care for education; that he did not wish to be a great man; that his desire was to be an Indian and scalp such persons as Mrs. Horr."[6] Jane Clemens sympathized with her son but was glad someone was finally able to control him.

Quarles's Farm

After moving to Hannibal, Jane Clemens missed her family and decided that Sam's health would continue to improve if he spent part of the year in the country at his aunt Patsy and uncle John Quarles's farm. The farm was located three miles northwest of Florida, Missouri. Jane Clemens made arrangements with her sister to take care of Sam. The first time Sam went to stay at the Quarles farm, his whole family went with him.

The seventy-acre Quarles farm "was a heavenly place for a boy" to visit.[7] There were trees to climb, eight cousins to play with, and a brook to wade in. One of Sam's cousins, Tabitha Quarles, or Puss, as her family called her, was Sam's age and his playmate. Mary, a slave girl who was six years older, watched over them.

The Quarles family owned thirty slaves. One of Sam's favorites was a middle-aged African American he called Uncle Daniel. He became Sam's "faithful and affectionate good friend, ally, and advisor."[8] Uncle Daniel played the fiddle and the banjo and sang black spirituals that Sam grew to love. He was also a storyteller and often, to their delight, scared Sam and his cousins with ghost stories.

Sam had a special relationship with his uncle John Quarles. Whenever Sam arrived, his uncle always greeted him with a hug and helped him carry his things. He also encouraged Sam to talk and to tell stories. Sometimes after supper he would ask Sam to tell about his day's adventures. Sam usually embellished his stories and often added a bit of humor. In time, he developed a talent for telling tall tales.

Once, a neighbor asked Sam's mother whether she believed anything Sam said. She replied, "I know his average, therefore he never deceives me. I discount him thirty per cent., for embroidery, and what is left is perfect and priceless truth, without a flaw in it anywhere."[9]

In the spring of 1842, Benjamin, one of Sam's older brothers, died at age ten. He was the third child Jane and John Clemens had lost. In their grief, they kissed. It was the first time they had ever kissed in front of their children. According to Sam's brother Orion, his parents were "courteous, considerate and always respectful" to each other, but they did not have a loving relationship.[10]

Boyhood Adventures

By his ninth year, Sam had grown into a healthy young boy with blue eyes, sandy hair, and rather large features. He was small for his age, and his head appeared too big for his body. When he talked, he spoke with a slow Southern drawl that his mother called "Sammy's long talk."[11]

Sam was full of mischief, found school boring, and often played hooky. He was the leader of a small pack of boys who liked to roam the hills around Hannibal. They pretended they were pirates, played war games, went skinny-dipping, or borrowed a boat to explore the river.

The most colorful members of the pack were Tom Blankenship, George Robards, and Arch Fuqua. Tom lived in an old run-down house near the Clemenses' home. He was the son of the town drunk. He never had enough to eat, wore clothes two sizes too large for him, rarely bathed, and did what he pleased. The other boys admired his independence. George Robards's long, straight, black hair hung below his jaw like a "pair of curtains."[12] He was envied by all the boys in the group, including Sam, who had curly hair. Arch Fuqua's unusual gift, admired by all his friends, was his ability to "double back his big toe and then let it fly" with a snap that "could be heard thirty yards" away.[13]

Sam and his friends had many boyhood dreams. When the circus came to town, they were all "burning to become clowns."[14] After the minstrel show left town, they all wanted to be entertainers. But, of all their boyhood dreams, they had but "one lasting ambition," and that was to be riverboat pilots, navigating riverboats up and down the Mississippi River.[15]

Mr. Cross

After completing third grade, Sam was enrolled in William Cross's private school. Cross was a middle-aged Irishman who had better than an average education. He lived up to his name because he was constantly short-tempered. Sam wrote a verse about him:

Cross by name and Cross by nature—
Cross jumped over an Irish potato.[16]

Sam was not a good student. He played hooky too often. But there was one thing he could do well. He was a natural speller. Every Friday afternoon there was a spelling bee in Cross's class, and Sam almost always won the contest. The winner was given a medal with the words "Good Speller" engraved on it to wear the following week. Sam wore his medal with pride and enjoyed being the envy of the whole school. Once, he did lose a spelling bee on purpose. He left the first *r* out of "February" so that his sweetheart, Laura Hawkins, could win.[17]

3

PRINT SHOP

Whyile living in Hannibal, the Clemenses were continually plagued with financial problems. They lost almost all their property to creditors, and Jane Clemens was forced to take in boarders. On March 24, 1847, John Clemens died of pneumonia, and his death plunged his family deeper into debt.

Within two years, Sam's mother could no longer afford to support him. At the time, Orion lived in St. Louis, Missouri, and was working in a print shop. Pamela supported herself by teaching music. Sam was nearly fourteen years old. It was time for him to go to work. Orion arranged for him to become an apprentice in Joseph Ament's print shop. Ament was also the editor of the Hannibal *Courier* newspaper.

As Ament's apprentice, Sam would learn the printing trade in exchange for room and board, and two new suits a year. Ament, however, was cheap. Instead of buying Sam a new suit, he gave him a hand-me-down suit. The jacket fit Sam like a "circus tent," and he had to "turn up his pants" to his ears "to make them short enough."[1] The second new suit never materialized.

Sam slept on a straw pallet on the print shop floor, along with Ament's other apprentices. The meals provided by Ament's wife were barely enough to keep them alive. Sometimes the boys stole potatoes and onions from the cellar, cooked them on the office stove, and ate them before going to bed.

While working in Ament's print shop, Sam joined the Cadets of Temperance. He made a pledge not to smoke or drink liquor and even tried to give up swearing. The main reason he joined the group was to be able to wear the organization's emblem—a red sash—and march in funeral processions and parades. His membership lasted for a short time. After marching in the May Day and Fourth of July parades, he resigned. He felt that it was too hard to "keep a juvenile moral institution alive" when a lad only had two occasions a year to dress up and wear the beloved sash.[2] After leaving the organization, Sam went back to his old ways and began smoking, drinking, and swearing again.

One windy day, Sam was walking down the street when a piece of paper flew by him. Intrigued, he chased after it. It was a page from a book about Joan of Arc. Sam wondered whether she was a real person. His brother told him she was a French heroine who had been burned at the stake. Sam was curious and read everything he could find about Joan of Arc. For the first time, he developed an interest in history and discovered the knowledge that could be obtained from books.

Orion's Newspapers

In 1851, Orion quit his job in St. Louis and moved back to Hannibal. He bought a printing press, hired his brother Henry as his apprentice, and started a weekly paper called the *Hannibal Western Union.*[3]

A short time later, he bought a daily newspaper called the Hannibal *Journal* for five hundred dollars. Then, he hired Sam to set type and promised to pay him $3.50 a week.

Samuel Langhorne Clemens, at the age of fifteen, is wearing his SAM belt buckle.

Joan of Arc

Joan of Arc was born in France in 1412. When she was thirteen years old, she began having religious visions and hearing what she believed were the voices of saints. The voices told her that God had chosen her to help King Charles VII drive the English out of France. By the time she was seventeen, Joan had taken command of the French armies. Within thirteen months, she led them to great victories, which paved the way for France's liberation from England. Joan was eventually captured, tried for witchcraft and heresy by church officials, and burned at the stake. In 1456, the pope of the Roman Catholic Church declared Joan innocent of the charges brought against her. In 1920, she was declared a saint.

Orion was impractical when it came to running a business, and he compounded his financial problems by trying to operate two newspapers at the same time. After buying the Hannibal *Journal*, he tried to create more business by reducing subscription fees and charging less for advertising. These two acts guaranteed that the paper would never make any money. In fact, Orion was unable to pay Sam a single dime for his work.

Even though Orion never paid Sam, he did provide him with the opportunity to begin writing. Sam wrote articles, humorous sketches, and poetry for Orion's publications. He liked to hide his identity and signed his works with various humorous pen names—Rambler, Grumbler, and W. Epaminondas Adrastus Blab.

Sam also liked to tease his readers and often ran items just to get their attention. In the May 6, 1853, issue of Orion's daily paper, Sam wrote the following announcement:

TERRIBLE ACCIDENT!
500 MEN KILLED AND MISSING!!!

We had set the above head [headline] up, expecting
(of course) to use it,
but as the accident hasn't happened, yet, we'll say
(To be Continued.)[4]

After operating his newspapers for a year, Orion felt the need to economize. He moved his printing press into the house where he was living with his mother, brothers, and sister. The house was small and his equipment "cramped the dwelling-place cruelly."[5] This only added to the family's misery. They were already living on a monotonous diet of "bacon, butter, bread and coffee."[6]

On May 1, 1852, Sam published his first humorous sketch outside of Hannibal. His magazine story was printed in a Boston weekly called *The Carpet Bag*. Sam continued to write for other publications and grew increasingly disenchanted with his brother. He was totally dependent on Orion and had to beg him for spending money. His sister Pamela had moved to St. Louis after marrying William Moffett, a successful merchant. Sam longed to travel and wanted to visit her. He also thought he might find a good job in St. Louis.

Sam confided in his mother and Henry that he wanted to leave Hannibal. Before he left, his mother picked up a small Bible and said, "I want you to take hold of the other end of this, Sam."[7] Then she asked him to repeat after her: "I do solemnly swear that I will not throw a card or drink a drop of liquor while I am gone."[8] She kissed him good-bye and told him to "write to us" while he was gone.[9]

Sam left Hannibal in May 1853. He was seventeen years old. After Sam left, Orion was unable to publish his daily newspaper for a month. Orion later admitted that he had not treated his brother well. He wrote, "I not only missed his labor; we all missed his bounding activity and merriment."[10]

On His Own

Pamela, her husband, and their ten-month-old daughter, Annie, lived in a boarding-house in a well-to-do part of St. Louis. Sam could not afford to live there, so he rented a

Samuel L. Clemens posed for this photograph in 1851 or 1852.

cheaper room in a boardinghouse that catered to college students. He found a job in the composing room of the St. Louis *Evening Star*. In a short time he was told that "his proofs [copy that has not yet been checked or corrected] were the cleanest ever set in that office."[11]

Sam stayed only two and a half months in St. Louis. Although he told his mother he was going to live there, he had no intention of staying. His goal was New York City. He longed to see the World's Fair that was being held in New York's Crystal Palace.

On August 19, 1853, he began a five-day journey, traveling by boat and train to New York City. He found an inexpensive room in a boardinghouse, changed his shirt, and set out for the Crystal Palace. He thought it was "a perfect fairy palace—beautiful beyond description."[12] He was also impressed with the machinery department that housed "all the world's newest wonders."[13] Inventions intrigued Sam, and he spent a lot of time looking at them. He wrote a letter home, telling about his adventure at the Crystal Palace. Orion printed it in the September 8, 1853, issue of the Hannibal *Journal*.

After a few days of sightseeing, Sam found a full-time job, working for John A. Gray & Green, the second largest book publisher in New York. He felt lucky to work there. He wrote home, "I will learn a great deal for they are very particular about spacing, justification, proofs. . . . [Y]ou must put exactly the same space between every two words, and *every line must be spaced alike.*"[14]

In October, Sam moved on to Philadelphia and took a night job working for the *Philadelphia Inquirer* as a substitute typesetter. Sam wrote home, telling his family about Philadelphia and complaining that he had not heard from them for some time. He knew Orion had sold his paper in Hannibal and suspected his family might have packed up and moved to St. Louis. Actually, they had moved to Muscatine, Iowa, where Orion had bought another newspaper and married Mollie Stotts, a young woman from Keokuk, Iowa. In November, Sam finally heard from his family.

In February 1854, Sam quit his job and made a quick trip to see the sights in Washington, D.C. He ran out of money after a few weeks and returned to Philadelphia, where he began working for the *Ledger* and the *North American* newspapers. He continued to write letters home about his travels, and Orion printed Sam's letters about Philadelphia and Washington, D.C., in his new paper.

In the spring of 1854, Sam was homesick and decided to visit his family in Iowa. He took a train to St. Louis to visit briefly with his sister Pamela, then boarded a steamboat headed for Muscatine, Iowa. He enjoyed seeing his family, but knew there was no future for him in Muscatine. A few months later, he returned to St. Louis.

Orion's newspaper was not doing well in Muscatine, and his pregnant wife, Mollie, longed to be closer to her family in Keokuk. In June 1855, Orion sold the newspaper and bought the "Ben Franklin Book and Job Office" in Keokuk. His mother, Jane Clemens, had already moved to St. Louis to live with Pamela, so only Henry accompanied them.

During the summer of 1855, Sam left St. Louis to escape the summer heat and visited Orion and his family in Keokuk. Orion offered him a job at five dollars a week plus room and board. Sam decided to stay, and once again the brothers were working together.

On January 17, 1856, Sam spoke at a printers' banquet held to celebrate the 150th anniversary of Benjamin Franklin's birth. After the program, Sam was "loudly and repeatedly called for" from the audience. He was not prepared but got up and gave a talk full of "wit and humor" and was "interrupted by long and continuous bursts of applause."[15] This was Sam's debut as a public speaker.

The Amazon

After eighteen months of living in Iowa, Sam grew restless. He had been captivated by William L. Herdon's and William F. Lynch's report, *Exploration of the Valley Amazon*, and longed to go to Brazil and see the Amazon River for himself. But he had one problem: Orion was not able to pay him most of the time, so he had no money to pay for the trip.

To finance his adventure, Sam made arrangements with the editor of the Keokuk *Post* to publish humorous sketches he wrote under the name of Thomas Jefferson Snodgrass. Then he moved to Cincinnati and went to work for Wrightson & Co., a printing company. He lived in a cheap boarding-house, saving every penny he could. On February 15, 1857, he boarded the steamboat *Paul Jones* and headed for New Orleans, the first stop on his journey to the Amazon.

4

RIVERBOAT
PILOT

When Samuel Clemens arrived in New Orleans, he discovered two things. There were no boats sailing for Brazil, and there probably would not be any for the next century. The route to Brazil had not yet been established. He was discouraged, and although he could have easily found a job in a print shop, he decided instead to pursue his long-lost childhood ambition of becoming a riverboat pilot on the Mississippi.

He had made friends with Horace Bixby, one of the pilots on the *Paul Jones*, and begged him to teach him to navigate the river. At first, Bixby rejected the idea because he felt cub pilots (pilots in training) were "more trouble than they're worth."[1] Finally, after three days of constant harassment, Bixby surrendered and agreed to teach Clemens the Mississippi River from New Orleans to St. Louis for five hundred dollars. Clemens borrowed one hundred dollars from his sister Pamela's husband, William Moffett, and agreed to pay the rest out of his first wages as a pilot.

Learning the River

Clemens thought it would be easy to navigate the Mississippi because the river was so wide. He had second thoughts, though, the first time Bixby gave him the wheel. Bixby told him to steer the steamship as close to nearby boats as "you'd peel an apple."[2] He wanted his cub pilot to learn how to navigate the crowded river. Clemens thought the steamship was too close to the other boats to begin with, so he steered the boat farther away from them. Bixby lost his temper, grabbed the wheel back, and scolded Clemens for being a coward.

In a short time, Bixby cooled down and began calling Clemens's attention to various landmarks as they passed them. Clemens thought Bixby was just making conversation, but during their next watch, Bixby asked him to name the first landmark out of New Orleans. Clemens replied that he did not know. Then Bixby asked him to name any of the landmarks he had mentioned earlier. Clemens could not name one. Bixby exploded. He called Clemens a "dunderhead." Then he added, "The idea of *you*

*Samuel Clemens grew up seeing steamboats along the Mississippi
River, and he dreamed of becoming a riverboat pilot.*

being a pilot. . . . Why, you don't know enough to
pilot a cow down a lane."[3]

After he calmed down, Bixby told Clemens he
needed to know the names of all the landmarks he
pointed out. He told him to "get a little memo-
randum book, and every time I tell you a thing, put
it down right away."[4]

Clemens obtained a ledger from one of the
clerks on the boat and in a short time had it "fairly
bristling" with names of towns, points, sand bars,
islands, and various other landmarks.[5] He was

beginning to get the hang of steering upstream when the boat arrived in St. Louis. Then he realized that he had "to learn this troublesome river *both ways*."[6]

In a few weeks, Clemens began to think that he might be able to learn his new profession. Then Bixby asked, "What is the shape of Walnut Bend?"[7] Clemens replied that he was not aware of any specific shape. Bixby lost his temper again. When he calmed down, he told Clemens, "My boy, you've got to know the *shape* of the river perfectly. It is all there is left to steer by on a very dark night."[8]

Clemens asked, "Have I got to learn the shape of the river according to all these five hundred thousand different ways? If I tried to carry all that cargo in my head it would make me stoop-shouldered."[9]

Bixby told him no, he only had to "learn *the* shape of the river . . . with such absolute certainty" that he could "always steer by the shape" that he had memorized in his head "and never mind the one that's before your eyes."[10]

Clemens never could get more than "one knotty thing learned before another presented itself."[11] Not only did he need to learn the shape of the river, but Bixby also expected him to remember the depth of the river in various places. This made Clemens furious, and he replied, "When I get so that I can do that, I'll be able to raise the dead, and then I won't have to pilot a steamboat to make a living. I want to retire from this business. . . . I haven't got the brains enough to be a pilot."[12]

Bixby told him to stop talking like that, saying, "When I say I'll learn a man the river, I mean it."[13]

Clemens made five runs up and down the Mississippi River with Bixby. During the summer of 1857, Bixby was offered a better-paying job, piloting on the Missouri River, and loaned Clemens out to work with other pilots. This was a common practice on the river. Bixby felt Clemens would benefit from the experience.

For several months, Clemens worked on the *John J. Roe*, a slow-moving barge that transported produce. While on the boat, he changed his hairstyle and grew muttonchop sideburns, fashionable among pilots on the river at the time.

Measuring the Depth of the River

In some places, the Mississippi River is only nine feet deep. In general, a riverboat needed to be in at least twelve feet of water so it would not hit bottom. Whenever a riverboat was entering shallow water, a crewmember called a leadsman would measure the depth of the water with a knotted rope that had a heavy weight on the end of it. He would throw the rope overboard and measure the depth of the river by counting the knots. If his line went down two fathoms, or twelve feet, he would yell out "M-a-r-k twain!" which meant safe water.

In February 1858, Clemens went to work for William Brown, a pilot on the *Pennsylvania*. Clemens later described Brown as a "long, slim, bony, smooth-shaven horse-faced . . . malicious, snarling, fault-finding . . . tyrant."[14] Brown would not allow his cub pilots to read while working for him and often lectured Clemens on the "ruinous effects of reading."[15] Brown expected his cub pilots to concentrate on the river and nothing else.

Henry

During one of his stops in St. Louis during the winter of 1858, Clemens visited his family. Orion had given up his printing business in Iowa and moved to Tennessee, where he intended to study law. When Orion left Iowa, Henry joined his sister's family and his mother in St. Louis. Henry was almost twenty years old and only working occasional jobs. Clemens wanted Henry to join him on the river and found a job for him on the *Pennsylvania* as a clerk. Henry's companionship made Brown's overbearing personality more bearable.

Clemens tolerated Brown's abuse until he called Henry a liar and struck him in the face. Clemens lost his temper, knocked Brown down, and gave him a good beating. Striking a pilot was close to mutiny, and Clemens thought he would be fired. When Clemens confessed what he had done to John Klinefelter, the *Pennsylvania*'s captain, Klinefelter did not even reprimand him. He felt

Brown deserved what he got, but told Clemens not to do it again.

Brown demanded that Clemens be put ashore and declared he would never pilot the boat again if Clemens stayed. Captain Klinefelter was perfectly willing to let Brown leave, but he could not find a replacement for him. To resolve the problem, Clemens was transferred to the *A. T. Lacy*. Henry stayed aboard the *Pennsylvania*.

One night, Clemens had a vivid dream in which he saw Henry's dead body. In the dream, Clemens saw Henry lying "in a metallic burial-case" set up on two chairs. He was dressed in one of Clemens's suits "and on his breast lay a great bouquet of flowers, mainly white roses, with a red rose in the centre."[16]

The dream worried Clemens, and before he left the *Pennsylvania*, he told Henry what to do in case of an accident:

> [D]on't lose your head. . . . But you rush for the hurricane-deck, and astern to one of the life-boats. . . . When the boat is launched, give such help as you can in getting the women and children into it . . . don't try to get into it yourself. It is summer weather, the river is only a mile wide . . . you can swim that without any trouble.[17]

Explosion on the *Pennsylvania*

Two days later, when the *A. T. Lacy* neared the landing at Greenville, Mississippi, word reached Clemens that the *Pennsylvania* had blown up, killing one hundred fifty people. That night in Napoleon, Arkansas, Clemens read the details of the accident in a newspaper. Four of the eight boilers on the *Pennsylvania* had exploded, blasting away the front of the steamboat. Henry was blown out of his bunk but somehow made it to the water and swam to shore. Then he swam back to the burning boat to help save the remaining crew and passengers. While he was helping others, he inhaled steam from the wreckage and "burned himself inside and out."[18]

For twelve hours, Henry had lain with the other survivors, exposed to the elements, on an island near where the boat had exploded. Finally, they were rescued and taken to Memphis, Tennessee. Clemens arrived in Memphis two days later and almost collapsed at the sight of his brother. Henry and thirty-one other scalded men were lying on mattresses in the public hall. They were "clothed in linseed oil and raw cotton" and every doctor and medical student in the area was caring for them around the clock.[19]

Clemens blamed himself for Henry's plight. He felt that if he had not fought with Brown and had stayed on the *Pennsylvania*, he might have been able to save Henry. For forty-eight hours, Clemens stayed by his brother's side. Around dawn on Monday, June 21, 1858, Henry died. A local resident, who had befriended the brothers, took the grief-stricken Clemens to his home to get some sleep. When Clemens returned to the public hall, he found Henry laid out just as he had envisioned in his dream.

Back to the River

It took Clemens several months to recover from the experience of his brother's death. In August 1858, he returned to the river and worked on several boats. On April 9, 1859, he was granted a pilot's license to navigate the Mississippi River between St. Louis and New Orleans. He began earning $250 a month, which was a "princely salary" at the time.[20] He sent part of his salary home to support his mother and brother Orion.

Clemens loved piloting on the river and took a great deal of pride in it. He felt a pilot was the only "entirely independent human being that lived on the earth," because when a boat was "under way . . . she was under the sole and unquestioned control of the pilot."[21]

Civil War

When the Civil War began in April 1861, the Mississippi River closed to nonmilitary traffic and Clemens's career as a riverboat pilot came to an end. He went home to Hannibal, Missouri, and, with fourteen of his boyhood friends, formed a volunteer Confederate army unit. They called themselves the Marion Rangers because they lived in Marion County. The loosely organized unit roamed the countryside, fishing and pretending to be soldiers.

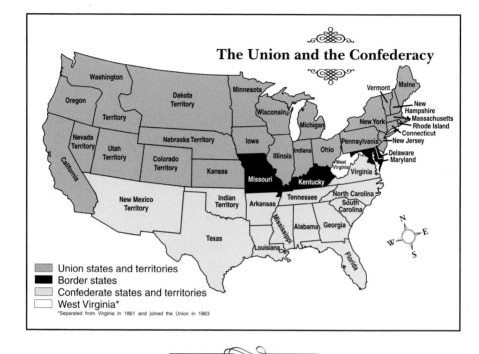

The Union and the Confederacy

Union states and territories
Border states
Confederate states and territories
West Virginia*
*Separated from Virginia in 1861 and joined the Union in 1863

When the Civil War began in 1861, Clemens was undecided about which side—the Union or the Confederacy—he should support.

After two weeks, the group disbanded when they heard reports that Union troops under the command of Ulysses S. Grant were approaching the town.

Later, Clemens jokingly wrote that, at the time, there was but "one honorable course for me to pursue and I pursued it. I withdrew to private life and gave the Union cause a chance."[22] Although he joked about it, Clemens could not decide which side to support—the Confederacy or the Union.

5

OUT WEST

In the spring of 1861, Orion was appointed secretary to the newly established Nevada Territory as a reward for supporting the candidacy of Abraham Lincoln for president in the election of 1860. The position paid eighteen hundred dollars a year. Orion was down on his luck and living with his in-laws at the time. He did not have the money to pay his way to Carson City, Nevada, where he was expected by the end of summer.

Clemens decided to accompany his brother on the trip west. He was afraid that if he stayed in St. Louis, he might be drafted to pilot a Union riverboat. Many people, including Clemens, thought the war would last only three months. He decided to go west until the war was over.

Orion appointed Clemens to the post of assistant secretary of the Nevada Territory. The job paid nothing and had no duties attached to it, but the title sounded important. In return, Clemens bought both of their $150 stagecoach tickets. On July 18, 1861, the brothers left St. Louis for St. Joseph, Missouri, where they began their twenty-five-day journey across the western plains.

Their stagecoach averaged one hundred miles a day and stopped only briefly for meals and to change horses and staff. Clemens called the stagecoach "a great swinging and swaying stage . . . an imposing cradle on wheels."[1] Clemens and Orion tried to sleep on their seats, but the dozens of mail sacks that had been crammed in their coach with them got in the way. Finally, they spread the mail sacks out along the floor of the coach and made a bed out of them.

One day during their journey, a Pony Express rider sped past them. At first, they could see only a black speck against the prairie sky. A few seconds later, the black speck took the shape of "a horse and rider, rising and falling, rising and falling," riding toward them.[2] Then, they heard the faint "flutter" of horse's hooves that grew louder as the rider approached.[3] The stagecoach driver shouted a greeting to the Pony Express rider, who waved and quickly "burst past" them.[4]

Pony Express
From 1860 to 1861, the Pony Express carried mail from St. Joseph, Missouri, to Sacramento, California, in ten days or less. Pony Express riders were usually small, young men who could travel light. They rode in relays, day and night, through all kinds of weather, over the 1,966-mile route. When the transcontinental telegraph began operating in October 1861, the Pony Express was no longer necessary and shut down operations.

Carson City

Around noon on August 14, 1861, Clemens and Orion arrived in Carson City, the capital of Nevada Territory. In a letter to his mother, Clemens wrote, "It never rains here, and the dew never falls. No flowers grow here, and no green things gladden the eye. The birds that fly over the land carry their provisions with them. . . ."[5] Carson City was in the middle of a desert in which nothing but sagebrush could grow.

Every day, usually in the afternoon, a huge windstorm would hit the little town. The wind was called Washoe Zephyr. Washoe is the nickname for Nevada, and *zephyr* means "west wind." Clemens said it was "something to see," and he would have liked to have seen more if he "could have kept the dust out" of his eyes.[6] When the winds died down, everyone was so covered with dust that they looked as though they worked in a starch factory.[7]

Clemens enjoyed the informality of life in the West and decided to stay longer than three months. He began wearing a damaged slouch hat, a blue woolen shirt, and pants crammed into his boot tops, and "he 'gloried' in the absence of coat, vest, and suspenders."[8] He also grew a mustache and beard and armed himself with an old navy revolver.

Get-Rich Schemes

Orion had nothing for Clemens to do, so Clemens decided to explore the countryside. After hearing about the land around Lake Bigler, which later became known as Lake Tahoe, Clemens found himself a partner, John Kinney, and set out to stake a timber claim and make his fortune. They explored the lake for several days and chose a two-mile area near a bay they named Sam Clemens Bay. Then they cleared the area, fenced it in, and built a cabin on the property.

One evening, Clemens built a campfire to cook their dinner and accidentally lost control of it. In a short time, flames were "galloping all over the premises!" In half an hour, the whole forest was in flames.[9] When the fire died down, the two timber tycoons were forced to return to Carson City empty-handed.

After returning to Carson City, Clemens came down with a bad case of mining fever. Prospectors were discovering silver all over Nevada. "I would have been more or less than human if I had not gone mad like the rest," Clemens said.[10]

Clemens tried his hand at mining in the Humboldt and Esmeralda mining districts. From December 1861 to September 1862, he worked various claims he had purchased with his brother and wrote numerous letters home to his family in St. Louis. Some of his letters were published in St. Louis newspapers and copies were sent to Orion in Carson City. Orion showed them to an assistant at the *Territorial Enterprise*, a newspaper in Virginia City, Nevada. The *Enterprise* reprinted the articles, and the editors encouraged Clemens to send articles directly to them.

Using the pen name "Josh," Clemens wrote several humorous sketches for the *Enterprise*. One of Clemens's sketches was about a man he called Professor Personal Pronoun. It had *Enterprise* readers chuckling all over Nevada. They quickly recognized the character in Clemens's sketch as Judge George Turner, the newly appointed chief justice of the territorial Nevada Supreme Court. Turner was a pompous young man who had a habit of continually praising himself.

Clemens had run out of his own money and was now depleting Orion's funds. He kept thinking that one of their claims would pay, but his situation was becoming desperate. He asked Orion to try to find him a job as a correspondent for the *Sacramento Union* in California or Carson City's *Silver Age*.[11] In the meantime, Joe Goodman, one of the owners of the *Territorial Enterprise*, offered Clemens a job writing for his newspaper.

Clemens hesitated. He still hoped to be hired by another paper as a California correspondent. When no other offers came through, he decided to head for Virginia City. He made the 130-mile journey on foot and arrived in the *Enterprise*'s office in September 1862. He was wearing a battered hat, a heavy beard, and his clothes were covered with dust. When someone asked him what he wanted, he replied, "My name is Clemens, and I've come to write for the paper."[12]

6

MARK TWAIN

Virginia City was located halfway up the steep eastern slope of Mount Davidson, on top of the Comstock Lode, the richest known silver deposit in the United States. The Comstock vein ran under the town, and miners worked twenty-four hours a day, blasting, picking, and shoveling. The frequent blasts often rattled windows and shook furniture.

Clemens reported on everyday life in Virginia City and also wrote humorous stories and hoaxes. By the spring of 1863, his sketches were being reprinted in newspapers up and down the West Coast, and he decided to start using a pen name. He talked to Joe Goodman, his editor at the *Territorial Enterprise*, and told him he wanted to sign his humorous sketches "Mark Twain." Clemens explained, "It is an old river term, a leadsman's call signifying two fathoms—twelve feet. It has a richness about it; it was always a pleasant sound for a pilot to hear on a dark night; it meant safe waters."[1]

The first article signed "Mark Twain" appeared in the February 3, 1863, edition of the *Enterprise* and was entitled "The Unreliable." In a short time, Clemens became known by his pen name. The West Coast papers liked the sound of it, and his friends started calling him Mark Twain instead of Samuel Clemens.

In December 1863, famous writer and lecturer Artemus Ward arrived in Virginia City on a nationwide lecture tour. Ward was extremely popular. President Abraham Lincoln sometimes interrupted his Cabinet meetings to read Ward's stories aloud. Ward liked Twain's work and predicted he would do great things. He also encouraged Twain to "leave sage-brush obscurity" and accompany him back to New York.[2] Twain was reluctant to leave the West Coast but did start submitting his work back east. The New York *Sunday Mercury* published several of his stories in February 1864.

San Francisco

Near the end of May 1864, Twain left Nevada because he had been challenged to a duel. The duel was a hoax staged by Twain and Steve Gillis, an editor from a rival paper. Dueling had just been outlawed in Nevada, and even though the duel never took place, Twain and Gillis were afraid of being arrested. They chose to flee and headed for San Francisco. The day after his abrupt departure, a Nevada newspaper wrote that Mark Twain "has vamosed, cut stock, absquatulated [left in a hurry]."[3] Both Twain and Gillis found jobs on the *Morning Call*, the San Francisco newspaper.

After the free-and-easy life in Virginia City, Twain found working on the *Morning Call* to be "fearful drudgery, soulless drudgery, and almost destitute of interest."[4] Twain became even more disenchanted with the paper when his editor refused to print an article he wrote about a group of men who attacked a Chinese man for no reason. A policeman had watched the violent incident and had done nothing to stop it. Twain asked his editor why he would not print the article and was told that the *Call* made its "livelihood

Mark Twain posed for this photograph after he arrived in San Francisco to write for the Morning Call.

from the poor and must respect their prejudices or perish."[5] The main subscribers of the *Call* were poor Irish immigrants who disliked the Chinese.

Shortly after this incident, Twain was dismissed from the *Call* and became the San Francisco correspondent for the Virginia City *Enterprise*. He wrote several scathing articles about San Francisco's police brutality. Twain found the Chinese "quiet, peaceable, tractable [obedient], free from drunkenness, and they are as industrious as the day is long" and he was appalled by the police's treatment of them.[6] In reprisal, the San Francisco chief of police sued the newspaper.

During the winter of 1864, Twain decided to give the San Francisco police time to cool off. He went to visit Steve Gillis's brother, Jim, at his cabin

Chinese Immigrants

Twelve thousand Chinese immigrants came to the United States to help build the transcontinental railroad during the 1860s. When the railroad was completed, many settled in California. In San Francisco, they were forced to live in a small segregated area called Chinatown and were often attacked by members of racially prejudiced political groups whose slogan was, "The Chinese must go!"[7]

on Jackass Hill in the Sierra Nevada Mountains. Jim was a gold prospector and master storyteller. While visiting Jim, Twain met Ben Coon, a former Illinois River pilot. Coon told Twain a frog story that caught his fancy. Twain wrote down an outline of the story in his notebook.

In the story, a man by the name of Coleman owned a frog that was especially good at jumping. Coleman bet a stranger fifty dollars that his frog could jump farther than the stranger's frog. The stranger did not have a frog, so Coleman went out to get him one. While he was gone, the stranger fed Coleman's frog small pieces of metal called shot. Coleman's frog was so weighted down that when the contest began, he could not jump, and the stranger won the bet.

In late February, when Twain returned to San Francisco, he found a letter from Artemus Ward waiting for him. Ward wanted Twain to write a story for his upcoming book. Twain began working on the frog story, which he called "Jim Smiley and His Jumping Frog." He completed the story too late to be included in Ward's book, but Ward's publisher showed the story to the editor of the *Saturday Press*, who published it in November 1865.

Twain's story was copied and quoted from coast to coast. The New York correspondent for the San Francisco *Alta California* wrote, "Mark Twain's story . . . has set all New York in a roar."[8]

At first, Twain thought his frog story was poor and was disappointed with the attention it brought him. In a letter to his mother he wrote, "To think that, after writing many an article a man might be excused for thinking [were] tolerably good, those New York people should single out a villainous backwoods sketch to compliment me on!"[9]

Twain had a change of heart when James Russell Lowell, a distinguished essayist, poet, and critic, called "Jim Smiley and His Jumping Frog" "the finest piece of humorous writing yet produced in America."[10] It could be said that Mark Twain "leaped into fame on the back of a jumping frog."[11]

7

ABROAD

Twain's problems with the police settled down.
After he returned from the Sierra Nevadas, he
lived in San Francisco for another year. During that
time, he continued to write for the *Enterprise*
and various literary magazines. In the spring of
1866, he was given his first assignment as a foreign
correspondent. The Sacramento *Daily Union* com-
missioned him to write a series of travel letters
about the Sandwich Islands, now called the
Hawaiian Islands. At the time, there was a great
interest in the islands' sugar, rice, and cotton indus-
tries. Twain wrote his mother and sister that he was
going to "ransack the islands" and "write twenty or
thirty letters to the Sacramento *Union*."[1]

Twain sailed out of San Francisco Harbor aboard the *Ajax* on March 7, 1866, and arrived in the city of Honolulu on the island of Oahu eleven days later. He was thirty years old and eager for adventure. An avid sightseer, he "went everywhere . . . saw everything, did everything, and wrote of it all for his paper."[2]

Near the end of his four-month stay on the islands, Twain met Anson Burlingame, the American minister to China. Burlingame was on his way to his post in the Far East, and his son Edward was traveling with him. Edward had heard about "Jim Smiley and His Jumping Frog" and wanted to meet Mark Twain. Burlingame sent a message to Twain, who later called on the diplomat and his son.

Impressed with Twain, Burlingame gave him some fatherly advice: "You have great ability; I believe you have genius. What you need now is the refinement of association. Seek companionship among men of superior intellect and character. Refine yourself and your work."[3]

Burlingame also helped Twain obtain an exclusive on one of the biggest news stories of the decade. Fifteen starving men from the missing clipper ship *Hornet* had washed ashore on the large island of Hawaii. The sailors had spent six weeks drifting across four thousand miles of open sea. Burlingame interviewed the survivors while Twain took notes. Twain stayed up all night to write an article for his newspaper. The following morning, it was sent aboard a boat that was leaving for San Francisco. On July 19, 1866, the Sacramento *Union* placed the article on the top of their front page and spread it out over four columns. When Twain returned to San Francisco, the *Union* gave him a three-hundred-dollar bonus for the scoop.

Sandwich Island Lecture

When Twain returned to San Francisco, he discovered that his *Hornet* article had increased his popularity considerably. He felt that he was "about the best known honest man on the Pacific Coast."[4] One of his friends, Tom Maguire, a theater owner, suggested it was time for Twain to break into the lecture circuit. Many authors supplemented their income by traveling around the country, giving lectures.

The idea appealed to Twain, but he was not sure it was the right time. He asked one of his editor friends, John McComb, his opinion of the idea. McComb encouraged him to go ahead and "[T]ake the largest house in the city, and charge a dollar a ticket."[5] A one-dollar admission charge was unusually high. Most speakers only charged a fifteen- or twenty-five-cent fee to attend their lectures.

Twain rented Tom Maguire's Academy of Music for the evening of Tuesday, October 2, 1866, and spent $150 on posters to advertise his lecture. The flyers were unlike anything the people of San

Francisco had ever seen before. Twain made some bold promises; then, in small print beneath his statements, he retracted them:

A DEN OF FEROCIOUS WILD BEASTS
Will be on exhibition in the next block.

MAGNIFICENT FIRE WORKS
Were in contemplation for this occasion, but the idea has been abandoned.[6]

At the bottom of the flyer he wrote: "DOORS OPEN AT 7 O'CLOCK" and "THE TROUBLE BEGINS AT 8 O'CLOCK."[7]

On the day of the lecture, Twain came down with stage fright. He was terrified that no one would come to hear him speak. He went to the theater early and sat backstage in the dark. The theater was "gloomy and silent," and Twain felt like a "doomed" man.[8] Then he began to hear people entering the theater. The noise grew louder and louder. Before he knew it, he was looking into "a sea of faces. . . . The house was full, aisles and all!"[9] Fifteen hundred people turned out to hear Twain talk about the Sandwich Islands. The lecture was so successful that Twain decided to hire a manager and go on a lecture tour of northern California and western Nevada.

Roving Correspondent

In December 1866, Twain left for New York aboard the steamship *America*. He was now working as a roving correspondent for the San Francisco *Alta*

California. On the first night of the journey, the ship almost sank in a storm. Then one of the passengers came down with cholera, an infectious intestinal disease that was often deadly.

The only positive thing about the journey was that Twain met Ned Wakeman, the ship's captain. The handsome sea captain was an excellent storyteller, and Twain found him "inexhaustibly interesting."[10] Twain wrote down several of Wakeman's stories in his notebook for future reference.

When Twain arrived in New York, he made arrangements to contribute articles to the *Sunday Mercury*, the *Evening Post,* and the *New York Weekly*. He also arranged for his story about the jumping frog to be published along with twenty-seven other sketches in a book entitled *The Celebrated Jumping Frog of Calaveras County and Other Sketches*.

In December 1867, the article he had written about the *Hornet* disaster was published in *Harper's Weekly* in New York. Twain was furious, though. Due to a typesetter's error, his name was printed "Mark Swain."

For several months, Twain tried to convince the editors of the *Alta California* to pay his passage on the first pleasure cruise from the United States to Europe and the Holy Land. (The Holy Land is a region on the coast of the Mediterranean Sea.) Henry Ward Beecher's Plymouth Church in

Brooklyn was sponsoring the excursion. The fare for the trip was $1,250, and the passenger list was limited to 110 people. Shortly after he arrived in New York, Twain learned from John Murphy, chief of the *Alta*'s New York bureau, that the paper had agreed to pay his passage on the five-month trip as well as twenty dollars for each article he wrote.

Before leaving on the cruise, Twain went home to visit his family. When he returned, he made arrangements for his New York lecture debut. He rented a hall at the Cooper Union for May 6, 1867. Unfortunately, he had a lot of competition that evening. Schuyler Colfax, the speaker of the House of Representatives, was giving a lecture; Adelaide Ristori, the great Italian actress, was performing; and a troupe of Japanese acrobats, jugglers, and magicians was in town. To fill the hall, Twain had complimentary tickets printed and given to local schoolteachers. On the night of the lecture, Twain appeared in full evening dress before a packed house.

Henry Ward Beecher
Henry Ward Beecher was an outstanding speaker and devoted abolitionist—a person who wanted to put an end to slavery. His Plymouth Church was based on the principle that "earthly success was God's reward for righteousness."[11] This philosophy appealed to many wealthy New Yorkers.

Quaker City Cruise

On June 8, 1867, a month after his Cooper Union lecture, Twain sailed out of New York Harbor aboard the *Quaker City*, headed for Europe. Mark Twain was one of the celebrities whose names were used to promote the cruise, along with Henry Ward Beecher and General William Tecumseh Sherman. A few weeks before sailing, however, Beecher decided to stay home and work on his novel, and the army sent Sherman out west to fight Indian wars. Mark Twain became the only recognized celebrity aboard, which made him uncomfortable. He was not used to having to be Mark Twain all the time. Sometimes he liked to hide from his public personality.

Twain referred to his fellow passengers as "pilgrims" or "innocents."[12] Instead of dancing their first night at sea, they had a prayer meeting and sang hymns. The *Quaker City* passengers were mostly devout Protestants, middle-aged, and wealthy. Many of them did not understand Twain's jokes, and he had little in common with them.

Although Twain spent a lot of time in his cabin, writing his travel letters, he did make a few friends. He developed a special friendship with Mary Fairbanks, who was traveling as a correspondent for her husband's newspaper, the Cleveland *Herald*. She was eighteen years older than Twain, and he called her Mother Fairbanks. She edited his writing and urged him to stop using slang words and raw humor.

Twain also enjoyed the company of his roommate, Dan Slote, whom he referred to as his "splendid, immoral, tobacco-smoking, wine-drinking, godless roommate."[13] Charlie Langdon, the seventeen-year-old son of a rich coal miner in Elmira, New York, also became one of Twain's favorites.

After crossing the Atlantic Ocean, the first stop for the *Quaker City* was Gibraltar, a British colony located on the northwest end of the Rock of Gibraltar on the coast of Spain. From there, the ship sailed through the Strait of Gibraltar, the passageway between northern Africa and Spain, into the Mediterranean Sea.

Twain wanted to see the Moroccan city of Tangier and decided to go there while a large group of the *Quaker City* passengers took a road trip to Paris. He was looking for a place that was "thoroughly and uncompromisingly foreign," and he found that place in Tangier.[14] He wrote to his mother and sister that the buildings and dress of the people were "strange beyond all description."[15] Twain bought a Moorish costume that consisted of a long, flowing robe; a red fez, or cone-shaped hat with a black tassel; and yellow slippers. He later wore the costume to a dance aboard the ship.

The next stop for the *Quaker City* was Marseille, a seaport on the coast of France. Twain took a train to Paris, the capital of France, and visited the Louvre Museum, where he saw "miles" of paintings by the old masters. He also visited the Palace of Versailles, which he thought was "wonderfully beautiful!"[16] While in Paris he went to a saloon and enjoyed watching dancers perform a wild dance called the cancan. During the dance, the women lifted their dresses as high as possible. Twain later wrote that he covered his eyes to shield himself from seeing the shameful act. He admitted, however, that he peeked through his fingers.

At noon on July 13, the *Quaker City* left Marseille for Genoa, Italy. From there, Twain and several of his friends left on a month-long tour of Italy. They visited Milan, Lake Como, Venice, Florence, Pisa, Naples, and Rome. They traveled at a grueling pace. They were up every morning at seven and did not go to bed until midnight. Twain was awed by the sights he saw in Italy. He was also outraged by the wealth and privileges enjoyed by church officials and royalty while so many Italians were desperately poor.

From Italy, the *Quaker City* sailed to Greece. On August 14, it reached the seaport of Athens. As a precaution against cholera, Greek officials quarantined the boat. One evening, Twain and several friends sneaked ashore and walked for two hours across vineyards and mountains to see the Acropolis. Twain called the old Greek fortified hill "the noblest ruins we ever looked upon."[17]

After leaving Greece, the *Quaker City* sailed to Constantinople in Turkey, then into the Black Sea, stopping in the Russian seaports of Odessa, Sevastopol, and Yalta. In Yalta, the passengers of the *Quaker City* visited Russian Czar Alexander II at his summer home. Twain wrote a brief speech that was read to the czar when they were introduced to him.

On August 28, the ship left Yalta and returned to Turkey. A few days later, while the *Quaker City* was anchored in the Bay of Smyrna in western Turkey, Charlie Langdon invited Twain to his cabin and

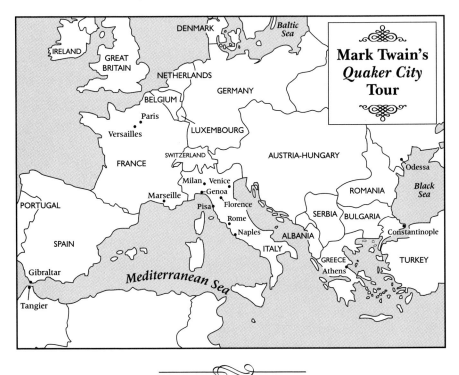

While on his tour with the Quaker City *group, Mark Twain visited cities in Africa, France, Italy, Greece, Turkey, and Russia.*

showed him a picture of his twenty-one-year-old sister, Olivia. According to a friend, Twain looked at her picture "with long admiration" and resolved "that some day he would meet the owner of that lovely face. . . ."[18]

From Turkey, the ship went to Beirut, Lebanon. Twain and seven other passengers left the ship and took a three-day trip through the Holy Land on horseback. The poverty, ignorance, and misery he saw while traveling through the countryside troubled Twain.

When Twain and his friends returned to the *Quaker City*, the ship made its final stop in Egypt, and then started on its return trip to the United States on October 7, 1867. The ship arrived in New York City on November 19 at ten o'clock in the morning. "The long, strange cruise was over, Amen," Twain wrote.[19]

Book Deal

When Twain returned to New York, he found that his *Alta* travel letters had been widely read. At the time, few

Olivia Langdon was the sister of Twain's traveling companion Charlie. Twain hoped to meet her one day.

Americans had traveled overseas, and they were eager to hear about ancient lands. Twain's letters were sincere, descriptive, and easy to read. On December 1, Elisha Bliss of the American Publishing Company contacted Twain to discuss turning his travel letters into a book. The American Publishing Company published subscription books. Their books were not sold in bookstores. Door-to-door salesmen traveled around the country, soliciting orders. When enough orders were obtained to ensure that a book would make a profit, then the book was published. Subscription books were large, highly illustrated books that usually cost more than the books sold in bookstores.

Twain had made up his mind that he "wasn't going to touch a book unless there was *money* in it, & a good deal of it."[20] Bliss offered him a choice between ten thousand dollars or 5 percent royalties. Even though Twain was almost broke, he decided to take the 5 percent royalty. This meant that for every book sold, Twain would receive 5 percent of the selling price. If the book sold well, he could make a lot more than ten thousand dollars. He later said it was "the best business judgment" he had "ever displayed."[21]

8

LIVY

Around Christmastime in 1867, Twain met the lovely young woman whose picture he had admired while on the *Quaker City*. He was in New York, attending a reunion of *Quaker City* passengers, when Charlie Langdon invited him to meet his parents and sister Olivia at the St. Nicholas Hotel. A few days later, Twain accompanied Livy, as Olivia's family called her, to Charles Dickens's reading at Steinway Hall. Dickens was one of Livy's favorite authors.[1]

The following day, Twain spent thirteen hours visiting the lovely and timid Livy at a friend's house. Before he left, he was invited to visit her in Elmira, New York, where her family lived.

For the next seven months, Twain was "too busy" turning his travel letters into a five- to six-hundred-page book to visit Livy.[2] He wrote at night and sometimes produced three thousand words in one sitting. In late July, he delivered his completed manuscript to Elisha Bliss in Hartford, Connecticut, and then went to Elmira to visit the Langdons.

The Langdons lived in a huge three-story house with grounds that covered a whole city block. An affectionate family, the Langdons said prayers and sang hymns together every evening. No drink stronger than cider was served in their home, and they did not believe in smoking. Twain enjoyed drinking liquor and smoking cigars, but he gave them both up while visiting the Langdons. The Langdons considered Frederick Douglass, a former slave and leading abolitionist, a friend. Before the Civil War ended with a Northern victory that ended slavery, they had supported the Underground Railroad.

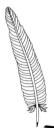

The Underground Railroad

The Underground Railroad was run by a network of antislavery Northerners. They helped runaway slaves escape from the South and make their way to freedom in the Northern states and Canada. Railroad terms were used to describe the secret network's operations. The operators of the network were called "conductors," their houses "stations," and the slaves they guided "freight."

At the time of Twain's visit, Livy's cousin, Hattie Lewis of Illinois, was staying with the Langdons. Hattie later wrote:

> My cousin Olivia and myself felt a little nervous about entertaining an unmarried man who had written a book! . . . We wondered . . . would he be funny all the time? . . . I really felt that I had one advantage over my cousin. . . . She was rich, beautiful and intellectual, but she could not see through a joke . . . unless explained in detail. . . . I soon discovered that my quickness at seeing the point of a joke . . . [was] simply nothing in comparison to my cousin's gifts. Mr. Clemens evidently greatly preferred her sense to my nonsense.[3]

Hattie also thought that Twain and Livy "would be a most suitable match" and cut her visit short so that they could spend more time together.[4]

Twain stayed with the Langdons for a week, and before he left, he proposed to Livy. She turned him down, but did agree to be like a sister to him. Over the next few weeks, Twain wrote many affectionate letters to "My Honored 'Sister.'"[5] Livy replied to his letters and told Twain that he was in her prayers. She invited him to visit her again at the end of September.

During his second visit, Twain intended to stay only a day and a night, but an accident lengthened his stay. While on the way to the train depot, he was thrown out of the back of the wagon in which he was riding. He was carried to the Langdon house and stayed three more days while Livy nursed him.

After he left, his correspondence with Livy continued. While visiting his friend George Wiley in New York, Twain confided that he was desperately in love with a beautiful girl, but she was too good for him. When tears came into Twain's eyes, his friend embraced him and told him to "Go for her, and get her. . . ."[6] Encouraged by his friend's words, Twain decided to "harass that girl and harass her till she'll *have* to say yes!"[7]

Twain visited the Langdons again in November. Livy attended his lecture entitled "The American Vandal Abroad," about his Holy Land excursion. For several days, she tried to avoid Twain, but then, on Wednesday night, she told him "over and over and over again that she loved" him and "was sorry she did and hoped it would pass away."[8] The following day Livy changed her mind and said that "she was *glad and proud*" that she loved him.[9]

Livy's parents agreed to their engagement as long as they kept it

In the early 1870s, this photograph was taken of three of America's most popular humorists, from left: Petroleum V. Nasby, Mark Twain, and Josh Billings.

secret. Jervis Langdon, Livy's father, wanted time to check on his prospective son-in-law's character. He asked Twain for a list of character references. Twain supplied him with the names of six prominent men he knew out west, two of whom were ministers.

Unfortunately, Twain's character references did not write complimentary things about him. They said he made "trivial" use of his talent, was "born to be hung," and would "fill a drunkard's grave."[10] After reading the responses to his inquiries, Langdon asked Twain, "What kind of people are these? Haven't you a friend in the world?"[11] Twain said that it appeared he did not. To this, Livy's father replied, "I'll be your friend, myself. Take the girl. I know you better than they do."[12]

On February 4, 1869, Twain and Livy became formally engaged. For an engagement ring, Twain gave Livy a plain gold ring that his friend Mary Fairbanks helped him pick out. The day after his engagement, Twain wrote to his family to inform them that "I was duly & solemnly & irrevocably engaged to be married to Miss Olivia Langdon, aged 23 $1/2$, only daughter of Jervis and Olivia Langdon, of Elmira, New York. *Amen.* She is the best girl in all the world, & the most sensible, & I am just as proud of her as I can be."[13]

Livy helped Twain edit his manuscript, and on July 20, 1869, *The Innocents Abroad* was published. Although subscription books were looked down upon and rarely reviewed, the book received an encouraging review from *Atlantic Monthly* magazine. William Dean Howells, the assistant editor of the magazine, wrote the review. Twain took the time to stop by the magazine's office to thank Howells. In a short time, the two men became friends.

Within six months, *The Innocents Abroad* sold eighty thousand copies. The book was priced at four dollars, and Twain earned royalties of about nineteen cents per copy. Twain wrote to Mary Fairbanks in Cleveland, "My book is waltzing me out of debt so fast that I shan't [shall not] owe any man a cent by this time next year."[14] Twain paid off the debts he had acquired while living in San Francisco and writing his book. He also sent a thousand dollars home to his mother and sister and bought a life insurance policy to benefit his mother in case something happened to him.

After becoming engaged to Livy, Twain went on a lecture tour through Ohio, Pennsylvania, New York, Michigan, Indiana, Illinois, Iowa, Massachusetts, Rhode Island, Connecticut, and New Jersey. During his numerous trips across the country, he stopped several times in Hartford, Connecticut, where his publisher was located. On one of those visits, he met the Reverend Joseph H. Twichell at a church social. Twichell invited Twain to tea at his home two days later. Twain liked Twichell's wife, Harmony, and had a "splendid" time visiting them.[15] The two men found they had a lot in common and even liked the same authors. Twain left carrying some of the "choicest books" from Twichell's library.[16]

At seven in the evening on February 2, 1870, Twain and Livy were married in the Langdon home. The Reverends Thomas K. Beecher and Joseph H. Twichell conducted the wedding. One hundred people attended the fashionable affair. The day after the wedding, a small group of family members and friends accompanied the newlyweds to their new home in Buffalo, New York.

Twain had expected to begin his married life living in a stylish boardinghouse, but his father-in-law surprised him with a generous wedding gift. He gave his daughter and son-in-law a furnished, three-story brick house, along with servants, a carriage, and a large check to pay household expenses. Twain thanked the Langdons for the generous gift and said he felt like "Little Sammy in Fairy Land."[17]

9

FAMILY LIFE AND WRITING

Shortly after his marriage, Twain wrote to an old friend from his mining days in Nevada. In his letter he commented that if all his married days were "as happy" as the last few weeks had been, then he had "deliberately fooled away thirty years" of his life.[1]

The newlyweds' daily routine was modeled after Livy's family life. They rose in the morning at nine and retired at ten in the evening. Before meals they said grace, and after dinner they read aloud to each other. They liked to read poetry, novels, biographies, history, and science. Livy was an attentive wife. She spoiled Twain with affectionate "kisses and caresses" in such abundance that she astonished him.[2]

Not long after his marriage, Twain signed another book contract with Bliss's subscription publishing company. He planned to write about his experiences in Nevada and California and borrowed the notebook Orion had kept during their journey out west. He also had a huge box he called a coffin sent to him from his mother's home in St. Louis. The box was filled with his files from the *Territorial Enterprise*. Twain planned to deliver the completed manuscript, which he called *Roughing It*, to Bliss by January 1, 1871.

During the summer of 1870, Livy's father became ill with stomach cancer. Twain and Livy went to Elmira to help care for him. Livy and her adopted sister, Susan Crane, sat with their father during the day. Twain relieved them for lunch and also sat with his father-in-law from midnight to four in the morning. Jervis Langdon died on August 6, 1870.

Livy was exhausted and overwhelmed with grief. In a letter to a friend, Livy wrote that her father had been her "back bone."[3] Twain wrote a eulogy for his father-in-law, calling him "a very pure, and good, and noble Christian gentleman."[4] After the funeral, Twain and Livy returned to Buffalo to await the birth of their first child.

A childhood friend of Livy's, Emma Nye, came to cheer her. During the visit, Emma died of typhoid fever. The following month, Livy almost miscarried. On November 7, 1870—a month early—Livy gave birth to a four-and-a-half-pound son. They named him Langdon Clemens. Langdon was small and frail, just as his father had been when he was born. Twain announced the arrival of his son in his newspaper and joked that Langdon would soon go out on the lecture circuit and give speeches about milk.

Shortly after Langdon's birth, Livy came down with typhoid fever and almost died. Twain decided to take his ailing wife and son back to Elmira to recover. They went to Quarry Farm, the home of Livy's sister, Susan. Twain had no intention of returning to Buffalo. On March 2, 1871, he put the house in Buffalo up for sale.

Quarry Farm

At Quarry Farm, Livy began to recover, and baby Langdon's health stabilized. Finally, Twain was able to get to work on his book. At first, he was not satisfied with his work. He worried that his new book would not be as good as *The Innocents Abroad*.

An old friend from out west, Joe Goodman, came to visit Twain at Quarry Farm. During his stay, Twain asked him to read several chapters from *Roughing It*. Goodman sat down and began to read. Twain pretended to be writing nearby but was actually watching Goodman as he read. After a while, Twain lost his patience and threw down his pen, saying, "I knew it! I am writing nothing but rot. You have sat there all this time reading without a smile. . . . But I am not wholly to blame. . . . I have been trying to write a funny book, with dead people and sickness everywhere."[5] Goodman replied, "I was reading critically, not for amusement . . . this is one of the best things you have ever written. . . . You are doing a great book!"[6] With his friend's encouragement, Twain pushed forward with his book. He wrote Bliss that he was writing "with a red-hot interest" and was turning out thirty to sixty handwritten pages a day.[7]

Hartford

At the end of the summer, Twain moved his family to Hartford, Connecticut. He intended to make it their permanent home. He felt that Hartford was "the best-built and handsomest town" he had ever seen.[8] He rented a house on Forest Street until he could build a home for his family. He was short of funds when he finished writing *Roughing It* and decided to go back on the lecture circuit to make up his losses and to promote his upcoming book.

The following summer, Twain took his family on a vacation to Saybrook, on the coast of Connecticut. Near the end of August, he sailed alone to England to do research for a book on English life and customs. While in England, he was treated like a celebrity. The British enjoyed his humor. Twain returned to America at the end of November, promising his hosts he would return on a lecture tour.

Twain and his family went back to Hartford during the winter of 1871. On March 19, 1872, Livy gave birth to their second child, Olivia Susan Clemens. She was a small baby, weighing just a little more than Langdon had when he was born. They called her Susy. Ten weeks after Susy's birth, Langdon died. He had never been a strong child. At the age of nineteen months, he had contracted diphtheria. He died on June 2, 1872.

Twain bought five acres of land on the western edge of Hartford in an area called Nook Farm and hired an architect to design a home for his family. Nook Farm was the literary and social center of Hartford. Harriet Beecher Stowe, the author of *Uncle Tom's Cabin*, owned the property next door. Her sister, Isabella Beecher Hooker, a zealous feminist, also lived in the neighborhood. So did Charles D. Warner, a novelist and the publisher of the Hartford newspaper the *Courant*. The parsonage of Twain's friend the Reverend Joe Twichell was also nearby. While the house was being constructed, Twain took his family to England with him on a lecture tour.

One winter evening in 1873, after they returned from England, Twain and Livy dined with their neighbors, Charles and Susan Warner. At one point during the dinner, their conversation turned to books. Twain and Warner criticized the quality of the novels their wives were reading. In return, the ladies challenged their husbands to write a better book.

The two writers could not resist the challenge. They agreed to write a book together. According to Twain, Warner "worked up the fiction" and "I have hurled in the facts."[9] The theme of the book was corruption. It was entitled *The Gilded Age: A Tale of Today*. At the time, many politicians sold their votes on important issues to the highest bidder, and businessmen bribed judges and other public officials. The book was published in December 1873. The following year, Twain turned it into a successful Broadway play entitled *Colonel Sanders*.

On June 8, 1874, in Elmira, Twain and Livy's second daughter, Clara Spaulding, was born. At birth, Clara weighed over seven pounds, and

In 1873 Mark Twain signed this photograph that was taken in London, England, while he was on a lecture tour.

Twain called her "the great American Giantess" because she was so much larger than his other children had been at birth.[10] Two-year-old Susy liked her little sister and called her "Bay" because she could not say "baby."[11]

In September 1874, the family moved into the new home. The three-story house had nineteen rooms and five bathrooms. The house was bizarre looking with its three Gothic towers, a balcony that looked like a pilothouse, and a porch that resembled a riverboat deck. A reporter for the Hartford *Daily Times* called it "one of the oddest looking buildings in the State ever designed for a dwelling, if not in the whole country."[12]

Twain and Livy settled down in their new home to a life of raising their family and entertaining. Their house was often filled with neighbors and guests. Twain liked to dance, sing, and tell stories to his visitors. Livy had a hard time keeping him in his chair during dinner because he liked to pace the floor while telling a story.

All the entertaining took its toll on Twain's work. There were too many distractions, and he spent little time writing. Twain soon settled down to a yearly routine of spending the summers at Quarry Farm, where he did most of his writing. Twain explained, "I can write better in hot weather. And, besides, I must be free from all other interests and occupations. I find it necessary, when I have begun anything, to keep steadily at it, without changing my surroundings."[13]

Study

As a surprise, Susan Crane built a study for Twain on her property at Quarry Farm in 1874. The building sat on a small hill about one hundred yards behind the Cranes' house. It was shaped like a steamboat's pilothouse and lined with windows. Twain was delighted with the room. That summer, he started working on a book about his boyhood in Hannibal, Missouri. He called the book *The Adventures of Tom Sawyer* and worked on it "until his tank ran dry," and then put it aside.[14]

Later that fall, William Dean Howells, now the editor of *Atlantic Monthly*, asked Twain to write something for the January issue of the magazine. At first, Twain declined, but he later decided to write a series of articles about his experiences piloting steamboats on the Mississippi River. His seven articles were published between January and August 1875.

Writing about his experiences on the Mississippi River inspired Twain to pick up *The Adventures of Tom Sawyer* again. This time, he completed the manuscript and asked Howells to read it. Howells wrote Twain, telling him, "It is altogether the best boy story I ever read. It will be an immense success."[15] In December 1876, *The Adventures of Tom Sawyer* was published by Elisha Bliss's subscription publishing company.

Mark Twain looks out his study window at Quarry Farm in Elmira, New York.

Storytelling

Twain's daughters took great delight in their father's storytelling abilities. They liked to put him on the spot and ask him to tell them a story about whatever objects or circumstances they gave him. Sometimes they would bring him a picture from a magazine and ask him to tell them a story about it. To make it more difficult for him, they would often cover part of the page "with their pudgy hands" to keep their father "from stealing ideas from it."[16]

Another Travel Book

In 1878, Twain was eager to write another travel book. He thought a walking tour of Europe would provide the material he needed, and invited his friend the Reverend Joe Twichell to join him. He decided to take his family to Germany in April and have Twichell join him during the summer.

In preparation for the trip, everyone in Twain's household began learning German. Rosa, the family's German maid, was asked to speak only German to the children. Little Clara would not even attempt to learn the language, but Susy tried her best. One day, in exasperation, Susy told her mother, "I wish Rosa was made in English."[17]

Twain and Twichell spent the summer tramping through the Black Forest and Switzerland. They walked most of the way, but occasionally switched to a train, raft, or donkey cart. Twain kept his celebrity identity secret and registered in hotels under his real name, Samuel Clemens. For once, he did not want to call attention to himself. Two years after their adventure, in March 1880, Elisha Bliss published *A Tramp Abroad*, Twain's third travel book. A few months after the book was published, Bliss died.

During the summer of 1880, Livy gave birth to their fourth child on July 26. They named her Jane Lampton after Twain's mother, but they nicknamed her Jean. Twain wrote to Joe Twichell in Hartford, announcing his daughter's birth. He also commented on his family's recent popularity poll. As far as Susy and Clara were concerned, Livy had been the most popular member of the household until Jean arrived. Now, Jean was number one; Livy number two; the family cats, Motley and Fraulein, numbers three and four; and Twain number five. Twain also commented that when the cats were kittens, he had been running "nip and tuck" with them in the family poll, but when the cats grew up, they outclassed him.[18]

In September 1880, after completing *A Tramp Abroad*, Twain started working again on a book he had outlined several years earlier. Entitled *The Prince and the Pauper*, the story was about a prince and a pauper (a poor boy) who secretly changed places. Susy and Clara were old enough to appreciate the story, and as he finished the chapters, Twain read them aloud to his daughters. Livy edited the manuscript, and the girls would let out a sigh whenever their mother marked for omission a passage they liked. The book was published in 1881 by Twain's friend James Osgood. Twain dedicated it to "those good-mannered and agreeable children, Susy and Clara Clemens."[19]

Back to the River

After writing the articles about his riverboat days for the *Atlantic Monthly*, Twain longed to visit his hometown, Hannibal, Missouri. He said, "I felt a very strong desire to see the river again, and the steamboats, and such of the boys as might be left; so I resolved to go out there."[20] James Osgood suggested that Twain travel the length of the Mississippi River and collect new material to use to expand his articles into a book called *Life on the Mississippi*. Twain traveled alone from St. Louis to New Orleans in the spring of 1882. There, he joined Horace Bixby, the man who had taught him how to pilot a steamboat, for the return trip to St. Louis. At the time, Bixby was the captain of the *City of Baton Rouge*.

After his trip, Twain wrote in his notebook, "The romance of boating is gone now. In Hannibal the steamboatman is no longer god. The youth don't talk river slang any more."[21] The steamboat had been replaced by the railroad. Still, Twain's memories of the river were good enough to complete his book. *Life on the Mississippi* was published in May 1883 by Osgood.

Mark Twain posed for this photograph in front of his former home in Hannibal, Missouri.

A New Publishing Company and *Huck Finn*

With the success of *The Adventures of Tom Sawyer*, Twain decided to write a sequel.[22] He wanted to use one of the characters he had introduced in *Tom Sawyer* as the narrator of a new tale. He felt that Tom Sawyer was unsuitable for the role and decided that the character Huckleberry Finn should tell the story. Twain wrote the first half of the book in 1876, then picked it up again in 1879, then 1880, and again in the summer of 1882. He finished *Adventures of Huckleberry Finn* a year later, but the book was not published until February 1885.

Twain felt there was a lot of money to be made in the publishing business. Since his former publisher, Elisha Bliss, had died, Twain decided to start his own subscription publishing company and publish *Adventures of Huckleberry Finn* himself. He hired Charles L. Webster as his business manager. Webster was married to Twain's niece, Anne Moffett. Twain named his new company Charles L. Webster and Company.

Grant's Biography

Twain was interested in publishing other writers' works in addition to his own. When he heard that Ulysses S. Grant, the former president and Civil War general, wanted to write an autobiography, he persuaded Grant to sign a contract with his new company. Grant was dying of throat cancer and desperately needed money to support his family.

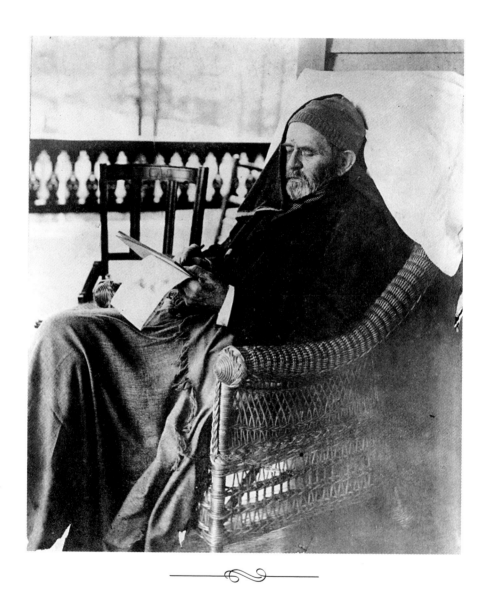

Ulysses S. Grant is seen writing his memoirs on June 27, 1885, at Mount McGregor near Saratoga Springs, New York.

Twain agreed to pay Grant a 20 percent royalty, twice what was normally paid to an author.

Grant's autobiography was entitled *The Personal Memoirs of Ulysses S. Grant.* Twain edited the manuscript himself. In July 1885, Grant completed the second volume. He died three days later. Sales of the first volume of Grant's memoirs went extremely well. Shortly after Grant's death, Twain was able to present Grant's widow with a royalty check for two hundred thousand dollars.[23] At the time, it was the largest single royalty payment ever made. In all, the Grant family earned more than four hundred thousand dollars from Grant's memoirs.

Papa's Biography

In 1885, Susy began writing a biography of her father. At the time, Twain was forty-nine and Susy was thirteen. Susy began her commentary by saying that "we are a very happy family."[24] Then she clarified that it was her papa she was writing about and that she would "have no trouble" in knowing "what to say about him."[25] Susy went on to describe her father:

> He has beautiful curly grey hair, not any too thick, or any too long, just right; A roman nose, which greatly improves the beauty of his features, kind blue eyes, and a small mustache, he has a wonderfully shaped head, and a profile . . . in short he is an extrodinary [*sic*] fine looking man. . . . He is a very good man, and a very funny one; he *has* got a temper but we all of us have in this family.[26]

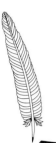

Cats

Mark Twain loved cats. As a child, he would take one or two of his favorite cats with him when he went to spend the summer on his aunt and uncle's farm. Twain's daughter Susy wrote in her father's biography that her family owned eleven cats. Her papa's favorites were named Sour Mash and Famine. In 1894, Twain wrote in his notebook that "If man could be crossed with a cat, it would improve man, but it would deteriorate the cat."[27]

Twain's children likened him to a spitting kitten whenever he lost his temper and threw a tantrum. His tantrums were common, and his daughter Clara once wrote that when her father's "performance was ended," she and her sisters would scold him and say, "Oh, you, bad spitting gray kitten!"[28]

In 1886, times were good and Twain wrote a friend, saying, "I am frightened at the proportions of my prosperity. It seems to me that whatever I touch turns to gold."[29] About this time, he became philosophical about his writing and wrote in one of his notebooks, "My books are water; those of great geniuses are wine. Everybody drinks water."[30]

10

DIFFICULT TIMES

After publishing Grant's memoirs, Mark Twain contracted with Generals William Sherman, Philip Sheridan, and Samuel Crawford to publish their accounts of their Civil War experiences. He also planned to publish a biography of Pope Leo XIII, the head of the Roman Catholic Church. Twain called the project "the Pope's book" and felt every Catholic in the world would have to buy a copy.[1]

Twain sent Charles Webster to Rome to obtain permission from the pope. The pope authorized the project and gave the book his blessing. He also gave Webster a rosary that he had blessed for Twain. When Webster returned, the rosary caused such excitement in the Clemens home that Twain remarked that he would not "take a thousand dollars for it."[2]

On February 12, 1886, Susy wrote in her father's biography,

> Mamma and I have been very much troubled of late because of papa, since he has been publishing Gen. Grant's book he seemed to forget his own books and work entirely, and the other evening he told me he didn't expect to write but one more book . . . he said he had written more than he had ever expected to . . .[3]

Inventions

In 1886, Twain's plans were to make his living by publishing other people's books and by investing in inventions. Twain was fascinated by technology and dreamed of making millions. With his background in printing, the Paige typesetter was the invention that intrigued him the most. He called it the "mechanical marvel."[4] The machine could set type five times faster and more accurately than human hands.[5] Twain declared that the typesetter made "all the other wonderful inventions of the human brain," such as the telephone, locomotive, cotton gin, and sewing machine, "sink pretty nearly into commonplace" and appear to be "mere toys."[6]

In 1886, Twain also began writing *A Connecticut Yankee in King Arthur's Court*, which he expected to be his "swan-song, my retirement from literature permanently. . . ."[7] The book is about a foreman in a Hartford gun factory, Hank Morgan, who is knocked

The Paige typesetter, in which Mark Twain invested heavily, could set type for printing five times faster than human hands.

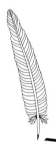

Calling Mark Twain

In the summer of 1886, Twain took his family to Keokuk, Iowa, to visit his mother and brother. For part of their journey, they traveled by steamboat. Their first night on board, Twain stood on the deck and listened to the leadsman call out the depths of the river. After hearing the leadsman call out "Mark twain" several times, Clara came running up to her father and said, "I have hunted all over the boat for you. Don't you know they are calling for you?"[8]

unconscious during an argument and wakes up in England during the time of King Arthur. Hank, like Twain, is fascinated by technology and tries to improve sixth-century society by introducing such technological wonders as lightning rods, printing presses, bicycles, and sewing machines. Twain was so intrigued with the typesetter and his new book that he wanted them both to be completed at the same time.

Bad Times

The next few years were difficult for Mark Twain. His publishing company was losing money rapidly. *The Life of Pope Leo XIII* barely made a profit. *A Connecticut Yankee*, published in 1889, was well received by American readers, but in England, critics attacked the book or ignored it because of Twain's negative portrayal of the monarchy. Twain was also sinking more and more of his money into the Paige typesetter. He kept thinking the machine would be perfected in three or four months and then the strain on his income would let up. The strain, however, did not let up. By 1890, Twain was spending three to four thousand dollars a month to keep "the cunning devil" of a machine going.[9]

Twain lost both his mother and his mother-in-law in the fall of 1890. On October 27, Jane Clemens died at the age of eighty-eight. Twain went to her funeral in Hannibal, where she was buried beside her husband. A month later, Livy's mother, Olivia Langdon, died at the age of eighty in Elmira. Livy attended her mother's funeral along with Susy and Clara. Twain stayed in Hartford with Jean, who had suffered a seizure caused by a mysterious illness that was later diagnosed as epilepsy.

Twain had invested nearly two hundred thousand dollars in the Paige typesetter by the beginning of 1891. His publishing company was plagued with poor management, and Twain continually had to pour money into the business to keep it afloat. In desperation, he cashed in all the stocks and bonds he and his wife owned and borrowed money from friends and family members.

Europe
In order to live more economically, Twain decided to move his family to Europe. Livy found new jobs for

most of their servants, had their belongings stored in a warehouse, and closed up their Hartford home.

Twain and his family sailed for Europe on June 6, 1891. While living in Europe, Twain was totally dependent on his writing to support his family. He worked hard and turned out several magazine and newspaper articles, even though he suffered from rheumatism. At times he could barely move his right arm.

After visiting several health spas, Twain's arm improved, and he began working on a historical novel about Joan of Arc. Twain intended *Personal Recollections of Joan of Arc* to be "his best and most important work" because it would not be humorous.[10] He feared people would not take the book seriously if the name "Mark Twain" were attached to it, so he wanted to publish it anonymously.

In June 1892, Twain made the first of what would be fourteen trips in three and a half years back to the United States to check on his business affairs. Despite his attention, his financial situation continually grew worse. When the stock market crashed in 1893, Twain lost all hope of finding more investors to help keep his publishing business afloat. Bankruptcy was staring him in the face.

Luckily, in the fall of 1893, Twain met Henry H. Rogers, an executive with the Standard Oil Company. Rogers was a fan of Twain's writing. After Rogers had attended Twain's lecture on the

Sandwich Islands in San Francisco, he had "read everything" Twain had written that he "could get hold of."[11] Rogers loaned Twain eight thousand dollars to keep his publishing business going and offered to help Twain resolve his financial difficulties by looking into the Paige typesetter and his other business interests. Rogers also told Twain to "stop walking the floor," which meant for Twain to quit worrying.[12]

Twain was grateful for Rogers's help and promised his wife that he would never try his hand at business again. He would make literature his life. He said: "I will live in literature, I will wallow in it, revel in it; I will swim in ink!"[13]

In April 1894, Twain's publishing company owed various banks and suppliers eighty-three thousand dollars and Livy sixty thousand dollars. Rogers convinced Twain that the best way out of his financial difficulties was to declare bankruptcy. In order to preserve Twain's personal assets, Rogers established Livy as the publishing house's main creditor and had Twain's home in Hartford and the copyrights to his books transferred into Livy's name. During the bankruptcy proceedings, Twain's creditors agreed to accept fifty cents for each dollar owed them, but Twain vowed to pay them in full. He still had dreams of the Paige typesetter making him rich.

His dreams were shattered in October, when the second model of the Paige typesetter was tested in Chicago. Rogers observed the test. When the typesetter broke down, he concluded that the unreliable machine had no commercial value. He wrote Twain, advising him that it was useless to spend more money trying to perfect the typesetter.

Because he could no longer rely on his beloved machine to save him, Twain believed the only way to pay his creditors in full was to return to the lecture platform. This time, he planned to do it on a grand scale and tour around the world. He also planned to write a book about his trip when he returned.

In May 1895, Twain brought his family back to the United States from Europe. They spent the summer at Quarry Farm, preparing for the tour. Susy and Jean decided to stay with their aunt Susan

Twain's three daughters—Susy, Jean, and Clara—sat for this photograph in 1891.

in Elmira. Twenty-one-year-old Clara planned to accompany her parents. On July 14, 1895, they departed from the Elmira train station. Later, Twain fondly remembered the sight of Susy standing on the train platform, waving good-bye. "She was brimming with life and the joy of it," Twain wrote.[14]

For thirteen months, Twain "lectured and robbed and raided" around the globe.[15] Everywhere he went, the lecture halls were packed, whether it was Australia, New Zealand, Ceylon, India, or South Africa. At times, the tour schedule almost overwhelmed him. In a thirty-eight-day period, he gave twenty-four lectures in twenty-two cities. Despite the hardships, the admiration of his fans kept him going.

While on tour, Twain decided to go ahead and publish his novel about Joan of Arc under his own name.[16] He felt certain that the success of his tour and the publicity he was receiving would help sell the book. Harper and Brothers published the *Personal Recollections of Joan of Arc* in May 1896. Harper and Brothers was not a subscription publishing house. It sold its books to bookstores. The *Personal Recollections of Joan of Arc* did not sell as well as Twain's previous books.

The world tour ended in Capetown, South Africa, a year to the day from when Twain started his tour. From Capetown, Twain sailed to England, where Susy and Jean were to join their parents. The day they were to arrive, Twain received a letter informing him that the girls had been detained. Susy was ill, and the trip had been postponed until her health improved. When no further information could be obtained about Susy's illness, Livy and Clara boarded a ship for home. Three days later, Twain received a telegram informing him that Susy had died. At the age of twenty-four, she had developed meningitis, a brain infection.

Susy was Twain's favorite daughter, and he later wrote about his feelings when he learned she had died. "It is one of the mysteries of our nature," he said, "that a man, all unprepared, can receive a thunder-stroke like that and live."[17]

Mourning

After Susy's funeral, Livy, Clara, and Jean returned to England. Twain rented a house in London and threw himself into the task of writing the travel book about his world tour. Livy lost interest in everything and refused to see anyone. She sat in her room alone day after day, mourning the loss of her daughter. Clara rarely went out and spent most of her time practicing the piano. Jean stayed home because her seizures had become more frequent, and her epilepsy was out of control. During this time, Twain once remarked, "My family are hermits & cannot see any one."[18]

On Christmas morning in 1896, the family ate breakfast together. No one mentioned that it was Christmas, and no presents were exchanged. The following July, on the first anniversary of Susy's death, Twain and Livy spent the day apart. They were in Switzerland for the summer, and Livy left the house early in the morning, without speaking to anyone. She rented a small room at a nearby inn and spent the day reading Susy's letters. Twain sat outside their rented house under a group of trees and wrote a poem in memory of his daughter.

Twain's seclusion led people in the United States to fear that he had died. A young reporter for the New York *Journal* was sent to Twain's home in London with instructions to write five hundred words if Twain were ill and a thousand words if he were dead. In June 1897, Twain made the following public announcement: "The report of my death has been grossly exaggerated."[19]

In June 1897, Twain's travel book *Following the Equator* was published. In a short time, thirty thousand copies were sold. The royalties from the book, plus the money Twain earned from the investments Rogers had made for him, enabled Twain to pay off his remaining debts. He was finally debt-free, which gave him "abundant peace of mind."[20] The news also brightened Livy's spirits, and she began to come out of her depression.

11

LATER YEARS

On October 15, 1900, Mark Twain returned to the United States a hero. He had survived bad times, done the right thing by paying off his debts, and started his life over. Newspapers all over the country called him "the bravest author in all literature."[1]

Twain decided not to take his family back to Hartford. Their house was filled with too many memories of Susy, and he was sure Livy could not take the emotional strain. He decided to live in New York City and rented a brownstone house in Manhattan, just a few blocks from his old friend William Dean Howells.

Mark Twain's name sold newspapers, and while he lived in New York, reporters constantly hounded him for his opinions on various matters. Clara once noted, "It always puzzled me how Mark Twain could manage to have an opinion on every incident, accident, invention, or disease in the world."[2]

Livy

Livy's health began to decline steadily. She suffered from a thyroid disease that was affecting her heart. In August 1902, she became critically ill and the family thought she was going to die. Doctors, however, were able to stabilize her condition. They prescribed complete rest, and for a while, Twain was permitted to see his wife for only a few minutes each day. Livy remained bedridden. In October 1903, Twain decided to take her to

Letters to Mark Twain
Mark Twain received letters from all over the world. Some of his fans were not aware of his exact address, so they addressed the letters to "Mark Twain, The World" or "Mark Twain, Somewhere" or "Mark Twain, Anywhere."[3] He was so well known and loved that the letters eventually found their way to him. Someone even sent a letter to Twain that was addressed "The Devil Knows Where." When Twain received the letter, he responded, "*He* did, too."[4]

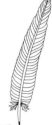

Florence, Italy, where the climate would be better for her condition.

In Italy, Livy continued to grow weaker. On the evening of June 5, 1904, she was talkative and cheerful while Twain sat by her bed for half an hour. Then he went downstairs to play the piano and sing the African-American spirituals he loved. Livy commented to her nurse, "He is singing a good-night carol for me."[5] A few minutes later she died.

Twain wrote to Henry Rogers, telling him of Livy's death. "Our life is wrecked; we have no plans for the future; she always made the plans, none of us was capable," he wrote.[6] "We shall carry her home and bury her with her dead, at Elmira. Beyond that, we have no plans. The children must decide. I have no head."[7]

After spending a night kneeling beside Livy's coffin, Twain wrote in his notebook, "I looked for the last time upon that dear face—and was full of remorse for things done and said in the 34 years of married life that hurt Livy's heart."[8]

After Livy's funeral, Twain moved back to New York City, into a house on the southeast corner of Fifth and Ninth streets. For a while, Jean lived with her father. Clara, who had helped nurse her mother through her long illness, checked herself into a sanitarium for a year's rest.

Lonely and depressed, Twain relied on his secretary, Isabel Lyon, to run the house and manage his social and business affairs. She also edited Twain's writing. Lyon, like most people at the time, did not understand Jean's epilepsy and convinced Twain that Jean was crazy and should live in an institution. Twain sent his daughter to a facility in upstate New York, a decision he later regretted.

On December 5, 1905, nearly two hundred members of the literary world celebrated Mark Twain's seventieth birthday at a banquet in Delmonico's, a famous New York City restaurant. William Dean Howells served as the master of ceremonies for the event. When Twain addressed the group, he talked about his nine-year absence from New York. "I find a great improvement in the city of New York," Twain commented.[9] "Some say it has improved because I have been away. . . . Others, and I agree with them, say it has improved because I have come back."[10] After five hours of speeches and toasts, each guest left the dinner, carrying a small bust of Mark Twain.

Twain's Biography

The following year, Albert Bigelow Paine, who had written about one of Twain's friends, political cartoonist Thomas Nast, approached Mark Twain about becoming his official biographer. When Paine called at Twain's home, he was taken upstairs to Twain's bedroom and workroom. Twain was propped up on his mahogany bed, smoking a cigar and writing letters. After Paine made his proposition, Twain was

Mark Twain is seen here, seated in his workroom.

quiet for a few moments. He had begun working on his autobiography several years before and knew his time was growing short. He wanted to finish the project. Finally, Twain asked, "When would you like to begin?"[11] The next week, Paine moved into a room adjoining Twain's bedroom.

On December 7, 1906, Twain traveled to Washington, D.C., to testify about copyright laws before a joint congressional committee. Twain, dressed completely in white in the middle of winter, made a dramatic appearance. He called his white suit "my don'tcareadamn suit" and wore it to express his freedom from social controls.[12] Now that Livy was gone, there was no one to monitor his behavior. Twain also had a passion for cleanliness, which his white suit exemplified.

Twain had almost always liked to be the center of attention, but in his later years, he seemed to crave attention even more. Sometimes he would walk down Fifth Avenue in his white suit and stop and talk to the police, just so people would stare at him. On Sunday mornings, he liked to go for a walk when the sidewalks were crowded with people returning home from church. With his white suit and bushy white hair, he was instantly recognizable.

As the years passed by, Twain felt isolated from his remaining family. Clara, who had made her singing debut in 1906, traveled a great deal, giving performances. Twain often quarreled with Jean, who spent most of her time in a rest home due to her illness. Twain missed what he felt was the idyllic time when his daughters were young. Because he had no grandchildren, he decided to adopt some. Twain formed friendships with more than a dozen young girls, whom he collectively nicknamed Angelfish after a beautiful fish he had admired in Bermuda, where he often vacationed.[13] Twain corresponded frequently with his young friends and even invited several of the girls and their mothers to be his houseguests.

In May 1907, Twain received a cable from the chancellor of Oxford University, in England, offering him an honorary degree. Earlier, Twain had said he would never travel across the ocean again. When he was offered the honorary degree, he changed his mind and told Paine he "would be willing to journey to Mars for that Oxford degree."[14] An honorary doctorate of law was conferred on Twain on June 26, 1907. His trip to England was a great triumph. He received overwhelming requests for personal appearances.

Twain's financial advisor, Henry Rogers, died suddenly of a heart attack on May 19, 1909. Twain was on his way to New York to visit Rogers when he received the news. In 1902, Twain had written that Rogers was "not only the best friend I ever had, but is the best man I have ever known."[15] Twain served as a pallbearer at Rogers's funeral.

In October, Clara married Ossip Gabrilowitsch, a concert pianist, in her father's home in Redding, Connecticut. Clara had named her father's new home Stormfield. Twain's old friend, the Reverend Joseph Twichell, who had officiated at Twain and Livy's wedding, married the couple. After the ceremony, Twain posed for photographs with his family, wearing his colorful Oxford gown over his white suit. Shortly after their wedding, Clara and her husband left for Europe, where they planned to live.

Soon afterward, Twain dismissed his longtime secretary, Isabel Lyon, after accusing her of embezzling

Mark Twain (left) wore his academic robes to his daughter Clara's wedding on October 6, 1909.

money from him. Jean returned home to act as her father's secretary. Twain called their relationship "a surprise and a wonder," because they were finally growing closer.[16] Two months after Clara went away, Twain wrote that it was hard to see her go, "but I could bear it, for I had Jean left. I said *we* would be a family. We said we would be close comrades and happy—just we two."[17]

Their companionship lasted for just a short time. On the morning of Christmas Eve in 1909, Jean was found dead. She had had a seizure while taking a bath and died of a heart attack. Twain was broken-hearted. On Christmas Day, he watched the hearse carrying his daughter's body leave his house in the middle of a snowstorm. Twain, who was suffering from heart disease and was too ill to attend Jean's funeral in Elmira, spent the next few days writing a tribute to his daughter. When he finished, he declared, "I shall never write any more."[18]

Twain's health grew progressively worse. He suffered from what he called a "tobacco heart" and attempted to cut down his cigar smoking from forty cigars a day to four.[19] He had difficulty sleeping and said that he had lost enough sleep "to supply a worn-out army."[20] In January 1910, he went to Bermuda for the winter. In Bermuda, he suffered several minor heart attacks and grew weaker. Twain worried that he would die before he could return home. In April, doctors suspected Twain's condition was critical and cabled Albert Bigelow Paine in New York. Paine sent for Clara in Europe and immediately went to Bermuda to bring Twain home.

When Twain returned home, he seemed to improve slightly. On April 19, he asked Clara to sing for him. It was difficult for her, but she managed to sing three of his favorite Scottish songs. Two days later, on April 21, Twain was napping while Clara sat beside his bed. Suddenly, he awoke, took her hand, and said, "Goodbye dear, if we meet—"[21] Before completing his sentence, he sank into a coma. He died around sunset that evening.

Twain had arrived in the world with Halley's Comet in 1835, and, as he had predicted several years before, he went out with the comet in 1910.

12

EPILOGUE

Dressed in a white suit, Mark Twain's body was placed in a coffin and transported by train to New York City. On the morning of April 23, 1910, a large crowd of mourners followed Twain's casket from Grand Central Station to the Presbyterian Brick Church on Thirty-seventh Street and Fifth Avenue. The church opened early so mourners could file by Twain's coffin and pay their last respects. The mourners represented every race, religion, and nationality. Hundreds lined Fifth Avenue, waiting their turn.

Twain's funeral service lasted only twenty minutes. Two ministers, Henry Van Dyke and Joseph Twichell, conducted the simple ceremony. The

THERE IS A TIME TO LAUGH AND THERE IS A TIME TO WEEP

This drawing of Uncle Sam kneeling at Mark Twain's deathbed appeared in a Baltimore, Maryland, newspaper on April 23, 1910.

Reverend Henry Van Dyke called Twain an honored man of letters and expressed his belief that "after many and deep sorrows," Twain was finally "at peace."[1] The Reverend Joseph Twichell could hardly hold back his tears as he bid his longtime friend farewell in a final prayer.

The following morning, Twain's body lay in state in the parlor of the Langdon family home in Elmira, New York. Later in the day, graveside services were held at Woodlawn Cemetery, where Twain was buried beside his wife and their three children. The Reverend Samuel Eastman, pastor of the Park Congregational Church, conducted the service.

Just prior to the graveside services, a large floral arrangement was received from an all-boy high school in Louisville, Kentucky. The card attached stated that the flowers were from all of the five hundred boys who attended the school. They were sent in memory of Mark Twain, who had "brightened their lives with innocent

These childhood friends of Mark Twain still lived in Hannibal, Missouri, in 1922, twelve years after Twain's death.

laughter and taught them squareness [honesty] and grit and compassion."[2] The flowers were a focal point near Twain's coffin during the services.

Clara Clemens Gabrilowitsch was pregnant at the time of her father's death. On August 18, 1910, she gave birth to a daughter, named Nina. Shortly after her daughter's birth, Clara and her husband returned to Europe, where they stayed until the beginning of World War I. In 1918, Clara's husband became the conductor of the Detroit Symphony Orchestra, a position he held until his death in 1936.

After her husband's death, Clara moved to Hollywood, California. Nina joined her mother and attempted to establish herself as an actress. She also struggled with drug and alcohol addictions. In 1944, at the age of seventy, Clara married Jacque Samossoud, a Russian musician and old friend of her late husband. Samossoud was a gambler, and he borrowed more than $350,000 from his wife, which led to financial problems. In 1951, Clara's Hollywood home and many of her father's valuable manuscripts and books were sold at a public auction. Clara died on November 20, 1962. Four years later, Nina died of a drug overdose.[3]

Legacy

Mark Twain's beloved friend and critic, William Dean Howells, called Twain "the Lincoln of our literature."[4] Twain was an unofficial ambassador of

Mark Twain is still remembered for the laughter he brought to millions with his writing and lectures.

goodwill for the United States, and his death was mourned around the world. In England, on April 22, 1910, *The Daily Mail* newspaper wrote that Twain was "the greatest humorist the modern world had known."[5]

In 1935, twenty-five years after Twain's death, Ernest Hemingway, another great American novelist, wrote, "All modern American literature comes from one book by Mark Twain called *Huckleberry Finn*. . . . It's the best book we've had. All American writing comes from that. There was nothing before. There has been nothing as good since."[6]

Today, Twain's books live on. So does the memory of the man dressed in a wrinkled white suit, holding a cigar, standing on a stage, making fun of the human experience to the delight of his audience.

CHRONOLOGY

1835—Born in Florida, Missouri, on November 30.

1847—Apprentices in Joseph Ament's print shop.

1851—Works in brother's print shop as a journeyman and as a reporter in Hannibal, Missouri.

1853—Leaves Hannibal in May; Works in St. Louis, New York City, and Philadelphia as a printer.

1854—Visits Washington, D.C., in February; Spends the summer with his mother and brother in Muscatine, Iowa.

1855—Spends winter and summer in St. Louis; Joins family in Keokuk, Iowa, and goes to work for the *Journal*.

1857—Becomes a cub pilot on the Mississippi River.

1858—Brother Henry killed in steamboat explosion in June.

1859—Receives pilot license on April 9.

1861—Outbreak of Civil War ends career as riverboat pilot; Goes west with brother.

1862—Joins the staff of the *Territorial Enterprise* in August; Starts using pen name, "Mark Twain."

1865—Short story, "Jim Smiley and His Jumping Frog," published in February.

1866—Travels to the Sandwich (Hawaiian) Islands on March 7.

1867—Leaves for Holy Land aboard the *Quaker City* on June 8.

1869—*The Innocents Abroad* published.

1870—Marries Olivia Langdon on February 2; First child, Langdon Clemens, born on November 7.

1872—*Roughing It* published; Daughter Olivia Susan (Susy) born on March 19; Son Langdon Clemens dies on June 2.

1873—*The Gilded Age,* written with Charles D. Warner, published.

1874—Daughter Clara born on June 8.

1876—*The Adventures of Tom Sawyer* published.

1880—*The Tramp Abroad* published; Daughter Jean born on July 26.

1881—*The Prince and the Pauper* published.

1883—*Life on the Mississippi* published.

1885—Forms his own publishing company; Publishes *Adventures of Huckleberry Finn* and *Personal Memoirs of U. S. Grant.*

1889—*A Connecticut Yankee in King Arthur's Court* published.

1891—Family moves to Europe.

1895—Family returns from Europe; Twain begins world lecture tour.

1896—*Personal Recollections of Joan of Arc* published; Daughter Susy dies on August 18.

1897—*Following the Equator* published.

1904—Wife, Livy, dies on June 5.

1909—Daughter Jean dies on December 24.

1910—Dies on April 21.

CHAPTER NOTES

Chapter 1. Life on the Mississippi

1. Mark Twain, *Life on the Mississippi* (New York: Harper & Brothers Publishers, 1883), p. 33.

2. Ibid.

3. Ibid., p. 34.

4. Delancey Ferguson, *Mark Twain: Man and Legend* (New York: Russell and Russell Co., 1966), p. 241.

5. Mark Twain, *The Adventures of Tom Sawyer* (New York: Oxford University Press, 1996), p. 30.

6. Ibid., p. 31.

7. Mark Twain, *Adventures of Huckleberry Finn* (New York: Oxford University Press, 1996), p. 2.

8. Ibid., p. 271.

9. Ibid., p. 272.

Chapter 2. Early Years

1. Margaret Sanborn, *Mark Twain: The Bachelor Years* (New York: Doubleday, 1990), p. 10.

2. Ibid., p. 3.

3. Ibid., p. 4.

4. Albert Bigelow Paine, *The Boys' Life of Mark Twain: The Story of a Man Who Made the World Laugh and Love Him* (New York: Harper & Brothers Publishers, 1915), p. 10.

5. Ibid., p. 14.

6. Ibid.

7. Mark Twain, *Mark Twain's Own Autobiography: The Chapters from the "North American Review"* (Madison: University of Wisconsin Press, 1990), p. 113.

8. Sanborn, p. 28.

9. Twain, p. 143.

10. Andrew Hoffman, *Inventing Mark Twain: The Lives of Samuel Langhorne Clemens* (New York: William Morrow and Company, 1997), p. 3.

11. Paine, p. 23.

12. Sanborn, p. 56.

13. George Will Sanderlin, *Mark Twain: As Others Saw Him* (New York: Coward, McCann & Geoghegan, 1978), p. 12.

14. Ibid., p. 11.

15. Ibid.

16. Mark Twain, *Mark Twain Himself: A Pictorial Biography Produced by Milton Meltzer* (New York: Thomas Y. Crowell, 1960), p. 4.

17. Paine, pp. 38–39.

Chapter 3. Print Shop

1. Mark Twain, *Mark Twain's Own Autobiography: The Chapters from the "North American Review"* (Madison: University of Wisconsin Press, 1990), p. 94.

2. Margaret Sanborn, *Mark Twain: The Bachelor Years* (New York: Doubleday, 1990), p. 68.

3. Andrew Hoffman, *Inventing Mark Twain: The Lives of Samuel Langhorne Clemens* (New York: William Morrow and Company, 1997), p. 28.

4. Sanborn, pp. 77–78.

5. Mark Twain, *Mark Twain Himself: A Pictorial Biography Produced by Milton Meltzer* (New York: Thomas Y. Crowell, 1960), p. 19.

6. Sanborn, p. 73.

7. Albert Bigelow Paine, *Mark Twain: A Biography* (New York: Harper & Brothers Publishers, 1912), vol. 1, p. 93.

8. Ibid.

9. Ibid.

10. Ibid.

11. Sanborn, p. 82.

12. Albert Bigelow Paine, *The Boys' Life of Mark Twain: The Story of a Man Who Made the World Laugh and Love Him* (New York: Harper & Brother Publishers, 1915), p. 53.

13. Ibid.

14. Sanborn, p. 84.

15. Hoffman, pp. 42–43.

Chapter 4. Riverboat Pilot

1. Margaret Sanborn, *Mark Twain: The Bachelor Years* (New York: Doubleday, 1990), p. 108.

2. Mark Twain, *Life on the Mississippi* (New York: Harper & Brothers Publishers, 1883), p. 45.

3. Ibid., p. 50.

4. Ibid.

5. Sanborn, p. 110.

6. Twain, p. 54.

7. Ibid., p. 63.

8. Ibid., p. 64.

9. Ibid., p. 65.

10. Ibid.
11. Ibid., p. 72.
12. Ibid., p. 71.
13. Ibid.
14. Sanborn, p. 123.
15. Ibid.
16. Mark Twain, *Mark Twain's Own Autobiography: The Chapters from the "North American Review"* (Madison: University of Wisconsin Press, 1990), p. 147.
17. Ibid.
18. Andrew Hoffman, *Inventing Mark Twain: The Lives of Samuel Langhorne Clemens* (New York: William Morrow and Company, 1997), p. 54.
19. Sanborn, p. 128.
20. Ibid., p. 130.
21. Mark Twain, *Mark Twain Himself: A Pictorial Biography Produced by Milton Meltzer* (New York: Thomas Y. Crowell, 1960), p. 39.
22. Mark Twain, *The Wit and Wisdom of Mark Twain*, ed. Alex Ayers (New York: Harper & Row, 1987), p. 42.

Chapter 5. Out West

1. Mark Twain, *Roughing It* (New York: Oxford University Press, 1996), p. 25.
2. Ibid., p. 72.
3. Ibid.
4. Ibid.
5. Albert Bigelow Paine, *Mark Twain's Letters* (London: Chatto & Windus, 1920), p. 41.
6. Twain, p. 160.
7. Clinton Cox, *Mark Twain: America's Humorist, Dreamer, Prophet* (New York: Scholastic Inc., 1995), p. 51.
8. Margaret Sanborn, *Mark Twain: The Bachelor Years* (New York: Doubleday, 1990), p. 161.
9. Twain, p. 176.
10. Ibid., p. 194.
11. Sanborn, p. 176.
12. Paine, p. 123.

Chapter 6. Mark Twain

1. Albert Bigelow Paine, *The Boys' Life of Mark Twain: The Story of a Man Who Made the World Laugh and Love Him* (New York: Harper & Brothers Publishers, 1915), p. 131.

2. Clinton Cox, *Mark Twain: America's Humorist, Dreamer, Prophet* (New York: Scholastic, Inc., 1995), p. 72.

3. Mark Twain, *Mark Twain Himself: A Pictorial Biography Produced by Milton Meltzer* (New York: Thomas Y. Crowell, 1960), p. 68.

4. Edgar M. Branch, ed., *Clemens of the Call: Mark Twain in San Francisco* (Berkeley: University of California Press, 1969), p. 282.

5. Ibid.

6. Mark Twain, *Roughing It* (New York: Oxford University Press, 1996), p. 391.

7. William Loren Katz, *A History of Multicultural America, The Civil War to the Last Frontier* (Austin, Tex.: Raintree Steck-Vaughn, 1993), vol. 3, p. 61.

8. Margaret Sanborn, *Mark Twain: The Bachelor Years* (New York: Doubleday, 1990), p. 268.

9. Delancey Ferguson, *Mark Twain: Man and Legend* (New York: Russell and Russell Co., 1966), p. 105.

10. Paine, p. 147.

11. Ibid., p. 146.

Chapter 7. Abroad

1. Andrew Hoffman, *Inventing Mark Twain: The Lives of Samuel Langhorne Clemens* (New York: William Morrow and Company, 1997), p. 102.

2. Albert Bigelow Paine, *The Boys' Life of Mark Twain: The Story of a Man Who Made the World Laugh and Love Him* (New York: Harper & Brothers Publishers, 1915), p. 148.

3. Delancey Ferguson, *Mark Twain: Man and Legend* (New York: Russell and Russell Co., 1966), pp. 109–110.

4. Margaret Sanborn, *Mark Twain: The Bachelor Years* (New York: Doubleday, 1990), p. 295.

5. Paine, p. 153.

6. Fred W. Lorch, *The Trouble Begins at Eight: Mark Twain's Lecture Tours* (Ames: Iowa State University Press, 1968), p. 27.

7. Ibid.

8. Sanborn, p. 297.

9. Ibid.

10. Ibid., p. 312.

11. Hoffman, p. 119.

12. Albert Bigelow Paine, *Mark Twain's Notebook* (New York: Harper & Brothers Publishers, 1935), p. 55.

13. Mark Twain, *Mark Twain Himself: A Pictorial Biography Produced by Milton Meltzer* (New York: Thomas Y. Crowell, 1960), p. 94.

14. Sanborn, p. 345.
15. Ibid.
16. Ibid., p. 347.
17. Ibid., p. 354.
18. Clinton Cox, *Mark Twain: America's Humorist, Dreamer, Prophet* (New York: Scholastic, Inc., 1995), pp. 99–100.
19. Sanborn, p. 373.
20. Cox, p. 102.
21. Ibid., p. 103.

Chapter 8. Livy

1. Resa Willis, *Mark and Livy: The Love Story of Mark Twain and the Woman Who Almost Tamed Him* (New York: Atheneum Publishers, 1992), p. 33.
2. Ibid., p. 36.
3. Ibid., p. 38.
4. Ibid.
5. Ibid., p. 39.
6. Margaret Sanborn, *Mark Twain: The Bachelor Years* (New York: Doubleday, 1990), p. 409.
7. Ibid.
8. Delancey Ferguson, *Mark Twain: Man and Legend* (New York: Russell and Russell Co., 1966), p. 142.
9. Ibid.
10. Willis, p. 42.
11. Ferguson, p. 143.
12. Ibid.
13. Willis, p. 43.
14. Justin Kaplan, *Mr. Clemens and Mark Twain: A Biography* (New York: Simon & Schuster, 1966), p. 108.
15. Margaret Sanborn, *Mark Twain: The Bachelor Years* (New York: Doubleday, 1990), p. 407.
16. Ibid.
17. Andrew Hoffman, *Inventing Mark Twain: The Lives of Samuel Langhorne Clemens* (New York: William Morrow and Company, 1997), p. 170.

Chapter 9. Family Life and Writing

1. Mark Twain, *Mark Twain Himself: A Pictorial Biography Produced by Milton Meltzer* (New York: Thomas Y. Crowell, 1960), p. 124.
2. Resa Willis, *Mark and Livy: The Love Story of Mark Twain and the Woman Who Almost Tamed Him* (New York: Atheneum Publishers, 1992), p. 60.

3. Ibid., p. 62.

4. J. R. LeMaster and James D. Wilson, eds., *The Mark Twain Encyclopedia* (New York: Garland Publishing, 1993), pp. 440–441.

5. Albert Bigelow Paine, *Mark Twain: A Biography* (New York: Harper & Brothers Publishers, 1912), vol. 1, p. 435.

6. Ibid., p. 436.

7. Justin Kaplan, *Mr. Clemens and Mark Twain: A Biography* (New York: Simon & Schuster, 1966), p. 136.

8. Twain, p. 130.

9. Ibid., p. 157.

10. Andrew Hoffman, *Inventing Mark Twain: The Lives of Samuel Langhorne Clemens* (New York: William Morrow and Company, 1997), p. 221.

11. Ibid.

12. Kaplan, p. 181.

13. Susy Clemens, *Papa: An Intimate Biography of Mark Twain* (New York: Doubleday & Co., Inc., 1985), p. 163.

14. LeMaster and Wilson, p. 12.

15. Paine, p. 548.

16. Clemens, pp. 88–89.

17. Albert Bigelow Paine, *The Boys' Life of Mark Twain: The Story of a Man Who Made the World Laugh and Love Him* (New York: Harper & Brothers Publishers, 1915), p. 214.

18. Ibid., p. 222.

19. Ibid., p. 225.

20. Kaplan, p. 242.

21. Albert Bigelow Paine, *Mark Twain's Notebook* (New York: Harper & Brothers Publishers, 1935), p. 165.

22. R. Kent Rasmussen, *Mark Twain A to Z: The Essential Reference to His Life and Writing* (New York: Facts on File, 1995), p. 228.

23. Ibid., p. 183.

24. Clemens, p. 84.

25. Ibid.

26. Ibid.

27. Mark Twain, *The Wit and Wisdom of Mark Twain*, ed. Alex Ayers (New York: Harper & Row, 1987), p. 33.

28. Clara Clemens, *My Father: Mark Twain* (New York: Harper & Brothers Publishers, 1931), pp. 84–85.

29. Paine, *The Boys' Life of Mark Twain*, p. 245.

30. Hoffman, p. 331.

Chapter 10. Difficult Times

1. Justin Kaplan, *Mr. Clemens and Mark Twain: A Biography* (New York: Simon & Schuster, 1966), p. 289.

2. Ibid., p. 290.

3. Susy Clemens, *Papa: An Intimate Biography of Mark Twain* (Garden City, N.Y.: Doubleday & Company, Inc., 1985), p. 187.

4. Kaplan, p. 281.

5. Andrew Hoffman, *Inventing Mark Twain: The Lives of Samuel Langhorne Clemens* (New York: William Morrow and Company, 1997), p. 349.

6. Kaplan, p. 281.

7. Albert Bigelow Paine, *The Boys' Life of Mark Twain: The Story of a Man Who Made the World Laugh and Love Him* (New York: Harper & Brothers Publishers, 1915), p. 259.

8. Resa Willis, *Mark and Livy: The Love Story of Mark Twain and the Woman Who Almost Tamed Him* (New York: Atheneum Publishers, 1992), p. 171.

9. Ibid., p. 169.

10. R. Kent Rasmussen, *Mark Twain A to Z: The Essential Reference to His Life and Writing* (New York: Facts on File, 1995), p. 255.

11. Willis, p. 211.

12. Paine, p. 272.

13. Willis, p. 216.

14. Kaplan, p. 333.

15. Willis, p. 225.

16. Rasmussen, p. 262.

17. Mark Twain, *Mark Twain's Own Autobiography: The Chapters from the "North American Review"* (Madison: University of Wisconsin Press, 1990), p. 26.

18. Willis, p. 242.

19. Hoffman, p. 416.

20. Kaplan, p. 350.

Chapter 11. Later Years

1. Justin Kaplan, *Mr. Clemens and Mark Twain: A Biography* (New York: Simon & Schuster, 1966), p. 358.

2. Andrew Hoffman, *Inventing Mark Twain: The Lives of Samuel Langhorne Clemens* (New York: William Morrow and Company, 1997), p. 434.

3. Albert Bigelow Paine, *Mark Twain: A Biography* (New York: Harper & Brothers Publishers, 1912), vol. 2, p. 565.

4. Ibid., p. 566.

5. Mark Twain, *Mark Twain Himself: A Pictorial Biography Produced by Milton Meltzer* (New York: Thomas Y. Crowell, 1960), p. 243.

6. Hoffman, p. 456.

7. Ibid.

8. Ibid.

9. Mark Twain, *The Wit and Wisdom of Mark Twain*, ed. Alex Ayers (New York: Harper & Row, 1987), p. 167.

10. Ibid.

11. Kaplan, p. 376.

12. Ibid., p. 380.

13. R. Kent Rasmussen, *Mark Twain A to Z: The Essential Reference to His Life and Writing* (New York: Facts on File, 1995), p. 14.

14. Kaplan, p. 381.

15. Ibid., p. 321.

16. Ibid., p. 387.

17. Delancey Ferguson, *Mark Twain: Man and Legend* (New York: Russell and Russell Co., 1966), pp. 317–318.

18. Kaplan, p. 387.

19. Ibid.

20. Ibid.

21. Clara Clemens, *My Father: Mark Twain* (New York: Harper & Brothers Publishers, 1931), p. 291.

Chapter 12. Epilogue

1. Andrew Hoffman, *Inventing Mark Twain: The Lives of Samuel Langhorne Clemens* (New York: William Morrow and Company, 1997), p. 500.

2. "Mark Twain at Rest; Buried Beside Wife," *The New York Times*, April 25, 1910.

3. Hoffman, pp. 502–503.

4. Mark Twain, *Mark Twain Himself: A Pictorial Biography Produced by Milton Meltzer* (New York: Thomas Y. Crowell, 1960), p. 289.

5. "England Feels His Loss," *The New York Times*, April 22, 1910.

6. George Will Sanderlin, *Mark Twain: As Others Saw Him* (New York: Coward, McCann & Geoghegan, 1978), p. 144.

GLOSSARY

astern—At or toward the back of a boat.

depression—A condition characterized by feelings of extreme sadness, dejection, and hopelessness.

destitute—Poverty-stricken.

drudgery—Hard, lowly, and tiresome work.

dunderhead—A stupid person.

epilepsy—A chronic disease of the nervous system, characterized by convulsions.

feminist—A person who believes that women should have the same rights as men.

heresy—Any opinion opposed to official or established views.

Holy Land—A region on the coast of the Mediterranean Sea that has religious significance for Christians, Jews, and Muslims.

journeyman—A worker who has completed an apprenticeship and learned a trade.

landmark—Any prominent feature, such as a tree or a building, that can be used to identify a particular place.

ledger—A book in which financial transactions are recorded.

monotonous—Repetitious or lacking in variety.

mutiny—Rebellion of soldiers or sailors against their officers.

pilot—A person qualified to operate a riverboat.

quarantine—Isolation or restriction on travel imposed to keep contagious diseases from spreading.

rambunctious—Boisterous and disorderly.

ransack—To search or examine thoroughly.

rheumatism—A term used to describe aches and stiffness in the joints and muscles.

rowdy—A rough, disorderly person.

scoop—An exclusive news story acquired by luck or initiative before a competitor.

swan song—A farewell or final appearance, action, or work.

switch—A slender flexible stick or twig used for whipping.

tall tales—Exaggerated stories.

tightwad—A stingy person; miser.

trivial—Of little significance or value.

villainous—Very bad, disagreeable, or objectionable.

wallow—To indulge oneself with unrestrained enjoyment.

wood shaving—A thin slice shaved off a larger piece of wood.

FURTHER READING

Books

Hakim, Joy. *Reconstruction & Reform*. New York: Oxford University Press, 1994.

Katz, William Loren. *The Civil War to the Last Frontier*. Austin, Tex.: Raintree Steck-Vaughn Company, 1993.

Meltzer, Milton. *Mark Twain: A Writer's Life*. New York: Franklin Watts, 1985.

Paine, Albert Bigelow. *The Boys' Life of Mark Twain: The Story of a Man Who Made the World Laugh and Love Him*. New York: Harper & Brothers Publishers, 1915.

Rasmussen, R. Kent. *Mark Twain A to Z: The Essential Reference to His Life and Writing*. New York: Facts on File, 1995.

Twain, Mark. *Adventures of Huckleberry Finn*. New York: Oxford University Press, 1996.

———. *The Adventures of Tom Sawyer*. New York: Oxford University Press, 1996.

———. *The Wit and Wisdom of Mark Twain*, ed. Alex Ayers. New York: Harper & Row, 1987.

Internet Addresses

The Mark Twain Association of New York, Inc. 1996. <http://www.salwen.com/mtahome.html> (December 10, 1998).

Robinson Research. *Samuel Langhorne Clemens, a.k.a. Mark Twain*. July 17, 1998. <http://www.robinsonresearch.com/LITERATE/AUTHORS/Twain.htm> (December 10, 1998).

INDEX